Talking with Your Aging Parents

TALKING WITH YOUR AGING PARENTS

Mark A. Edinberg

Shambhala
Boston
1988

To Daniel

SHAMBHALA PUBLICATIONS, INC.
HORTICULTURAL HALL
300 MASSACHUSETTS AVENUE
BOSTON, MASSACHUSETTS 02115

9 8 7 6 5 4 3 2 1

FIRST PAPERBACK EDITION

Printed in the United States of America

Distributed in the United States by Random House and in Canada by Random House of Canada Ltd. The Library of Congress catalogues the original hardcover edition of this work as follows:

Edinberg, Mark A.
  Talking with your aging parents.
  Includes index.
  1. Parents, Aged—United States—Family
relationships. 2. Parents, Aged—Care—United States.
3. Adult children—United States—Family relationships.
4. Interpersonal communication—United States.
I. Title.
HQ1063.6.E35   1987   306.8'7   86-29826
ISBN 0-87773-390-2   0-87773-440-2 (pbk)

CONTENTS

CONTENTS

ACKNOWLEDGMENTS

The following people were particularly helpful in the preparation of this book. I appreciate the interest, time, support, and thought each of them contributed.

Sia Arnason
Audrey Bernstein
Kathy Brennan
Mary Chacho
Gail Chotiner
Kendra Crossen
Barbara Edinberg
Barbara Felton
Maxine Goldstein
Patrick Henry
Melanie Kooris
Geoffrey Kooris
Margaret Kane
Clifford Laube
Ellen Mahoney
Katinka Matson
Emily Hilburn Sell
Judith Sugarman
Richard Wallace
Doris Wilhousky

I also wish to acknowledge my gratitude to Virginia Satir for her teachings, humanity, and wisdom about families; and to Barbara, Daniel, and Joel Edinberg for theirs.

1
An Introduction

Gloria and Jim are a couple in their fifties. Their children have grown up and are out on their own. Jim has worked for a corporation in New York for twenty years and is beginning to think about retiring in a few years and moving to Florida, where they have spent time every winter. Both Gloria's and Jim's mothers are living.

Gloria's mother lives in Philadelphia, is well off and very independent, but doesn't take care of herself as well as Gloria feels she should. Her mother lives in an area of the city that is not all that safe, she does not buy new clothes until her old ones are practically worn out, and she refuses to go to the doctor until her health problems are "really bothering her." Gloria dreads talking to her mother about any of these things, as her brother and two sisters who live nearby continually tell her that her mother wants nothing to do with any ideas from her children. But Gloria feels that, with enough encouragement, her mother would at least move to a better neighborhood.

Jim's mother is in a different situation. She lives near Jim and Gloria. Jim is her only son. Jim's mother, Clara, is also a widow, in her late seventies, but her health is failing. She is diabetic, has had a stroke, and has considerable difficulty walking. Gloria spends a good deal of the week caring for Clara, taking her shopping and to the doctor, cooking meals, and talking with her on the telephone at least once a day. Jim, who never felt particularly close to his mother, has a hard time being with her. He tries to reassure her about her financial status, which is precarious but adequate, at least for the present. Jim also knows that one of the major concerns his father had was that Clara would end up in a nursing home if he died before her.

Both Jim and Gloria know that when the time comes for them to retire, there will be adjustments on everyone's part. Should they continue living in New Jersey and taking care of Clara, whose health is questionable enough that her family physician has recommended that they consider a nursing home placement in the next year? How much influence should they have in Gloria's mother's affairs, even though they live some distance from Philadelphia and other family members are involved? And finally, how and when should Jim and Gloria discuss all of these issues with their mothers?

Jim and Gloria are a composite of people I have met professionally, in airplanes, in restaurants, or at social gatherings. They are decent, responsible people who are struggling with complicated issues about their own lives and the lives of their parents, trying to find ways out of heart-wrenching situations brought on by a combination of old patterns of family interaction, current needs in their own lives, and concerns about the circumstances of their aging parents. They do not know exactly what to do about their concerns; they do not know where to go for help or even what type of help is needed. We all know Jims and Glorias; they may be younger, they may have varying circumstances, but their struggles are universal. The struggles of Gloria and Jim and the struggles of others like them are behind the writing of this book.

WHY DO YOU NEED A BOOK ABOUT TALKING WITH YOUR PARENTS?

Around 1970, whenever I explained to people whom I met socially that I worked with the elderly, they would usually smile at me in bewilderment, seeming to express the unspoken thought "How can he stand it?" or perhaps "Why does he bother?" Times—and people's responses —have changed since then. I no longer tell new acquaintances that I work with the elderly—unless I have a half-hour free for the inevitable discussion of the problems they are having with their own parents or in-laws.

One reason for the change is that people are discovering a fact that has been known to demographers for some time: our population is aging. Perhaps more important than knowing that 25 million people (about 12 percent of the population) are elderly is the fact that people over age 75 are the fastest-growing (in terms of percentages) group of the population. A related result of the changes is that as "we" middle-aged persons reach age 65, there is a very good likelihood that at least one of our parents will be living. Not only are we aging, but our parents are aging and will be aged when many of *us* reach the beginning of what has been called old age.

Our nation is composed of people who have strong ties to their older relatives, despite the belief that old people are usually abandoned by their families. Families are increasingly involved in providing many types of assistance to their older members, including transportation, help with household chores, having an older relative moving in, emotional support, financial assistance, and help in obtaining benefits and needed services. Families are also becoming involved in difficult decisions, such as nursing home placement, finding adequate medical care, accepting difficult diagnoses, or deciding how an older relative with a terminal illness will spend his or her last days.

At the same time, I have been struck by the difficulties children of aged parents have in discussing these topics with their parents. Not only is it hard to raise the issue, but children often think that their parents cannot change, won't listen, or resist advice. In addition, there may be historical conflicts that affect discussions about current concerns.

The first reason, then, for this book is that with aging, there is a range of important issues related to your parents' well-being that need to be acted on but are often difficult to raise and discuss. In some families, for understandable reasons, the issues remain undiscussed, often leading to undesirable consequences. In others, these matters are handled directly, not without pain, but at least important information is given and discussed, and feelings can be shared and not get in the way of the good of all family members. The following stories illustrate these differences.

> Rebecca, a widow aged 75, had been considering leaving her house of twenty-five years for a smaller apartment. However, her daughter, Marilyn, felt obligated to have her mother move in with her. Whenever Rebecca talked about the need for other housing, Marilyn would say, "Mom, you can always move in with us," which was an option neither of them really wanted. Rather than "insult" her daughter, Rebecca stayed in her own home much longer than she wished to.

> Jean had been widowed only a short time. Her daughter, Katherine, and her son-in-law, Peter, thought that it would be best for Jean to move in with them and sincerely wanted her to. Jean, on the other hand, wanted to stay by herself, even though she knew that Katherine and Peter were worried about her being alone. Both Katherine and Jean were able to talk about the situation in terms of what they wanted for themselves as well as concerns they had for each other. Jean stayed in her home. Katherine was somewhat concerned, but she also knew that her mother was making a choice to stay on her own and could respect the decision.

These two situations have several important points to consider. One is that having direct or "open" communication with your parents does *not* guarantee that they will do what *you* want them to do, as was the case with Katherine and Jean. However, knowing each other's wishes and concerns can help both you and your parents appreciate each other's position and decrease guilt, blame, or other hard and negative feelings. In addition, if concerns and wishes are not made explicit, then decisions like Rebecca's, which was not what anyone wanted, may end up taking place.

A second reason for this book is that talking with your parents can lead to better understanding and appreciation on both sides. Even if there are no changes (as was the case for Katherine and Jean), communication and understanding can decrease guilt, a sense of burden, or other uncomfortable feelings we too often carry about our obligations to older relatives.

And, if there is misunderstanding, low trust, or discomfort on your side of the relationship, rest assured that your parent has some of the same feelings. Not only do children feel that their parents won't discuss certain issues, but older parents believe that their children avoid some of the same issues. I have, upon occasion, gone out and given "You and Your Middle-Aged Children" workshops at senior centers. I frequently ask the group, "What are the topics your families have most difficulty discussing with you?" These topics, in part, form the basis of this book.

Talking about important matters is not necessarily easy, but, again, it is one way to set the record straight. In fact, by honestly and directly discussing important matters about the well-being of your parents with them, you can make peace about other matters in your family's past, which is a third reason for reading and using this book.

In any family, there are pieces of history and events that still can raise unpleasant feelings on the part of all members. It is never too late to find new meaning and understanding about incidents in the past. We cannot change history, but we can change how we feel and think about it. Although the focus of this book is more on how you can talk to your parents about current matters than on rewriting your past, I firmly believe that the better your sense of shared history and peace is, the easier it will be to talk about current matters. At the same time, working directly on current matters can lead to a better appreciation and understanding of past emotional baggage.

There is a fourth reason for this book, one that is captured in the following story:

Once, long ago, there was a farmer, who, when his father had reached 70 years of age (a very ripe old age in those days), knew the old man was no longer productive and it was time to send him out to the barn to live, where he would most certainly die from exposure and lack of food. The farmer, being a gentle sort in his own way, called for his son and told him to bring the old man out to the barn with a meager blanket to cover him. After about fifteen minutes the son returned, carrying half of the blanket. The farmer, aghast at what he saw, asked, "Why did you leave that poor old man out there with only half of a blanket to cover him?"

"Father, I felt it important to save some of the blanket for you," the son replied.

The fourth reason, then, as illustrated by this story, is our own self-interest. As we handle the difficulties many of our older relatives are facing, we are showing our younger family members how to handle the future problems of their elderly parents—us! Rest assured that if you cannot talk to your parents about their health, wealth, or living arrangements, it is more than likely that your own children or the people who will be taking care of you in your old age will have the same difficulties talking with you, unless both of you make some changes between now and then.

These four reasons—helping your parents get what they need, working for better understanding of the present, straightening out the past, and ensuring a better future—are why this book was written.

What This Book Is Not

This book is not a guide about how to find and utilize services for older persons. Neither is it a text describing the many clinical conditions needing professional help, although some information is given about the common concerns along with ideas on where to go for more information or assistance. There are other publications that focus on finding needed services and professional help and on the clinical conditions (both mental and physical) that may be found in our older relatives. A good sample of these is listed at the end of various chapters.

In addition, this is not a book that can be followed by rote, with a guarantee of success in handling all of the problems with your older relatives. Our individual situations are too varied and depend too much on both ourselves and our older relatives to make any such "cookbook" approach useful.

What This Book Is

This book is a guide for all family members in handling important yet frequently difficult discussions with your older relatives. It is meant for any family member, regardless of sex, race, class, and educational level. I myself, as well as my professional colleagues, have had difficulty at times raising issues such as health changes or a need to have an older relative move in (or not move in). We all, as a culture, are faced with caring for older relatives in their seventies, eighties, and nineties who have varying needs and abilities to communicate and understand us. How we communicate with them will affect both the outcome of our discussions and how we feel about ourselves for having made the attempts to care.

This book is also a beginning point. It focuses on how to begin to discuss the feelings, thoughts, and concerns we have for our parents as they age. Beginnings do not guarantee what the ending will be. Things may work out quite well for you in talking with your parents or they may not. I attempt to put in warning signs throughout the book to let you know when things are getting out of hand and something else needs to be done, like stopping the discussion, bringing in someone else to help the discussion, or getting you (and ideally your parent) to a family counselor to try to make things work better.

This book is also about risk and change. It is risky business to venture into potentially turbulent waters, like discussions of death, family history, or even the fact that you are not going to visit next Sunday. Make no mistake about it, there is no guarantee that everything you discuss will be well received. However, the potential is always there for better understanding, appreciation, and personal growth. Because of the risks and "newness" of this approach for some readers, I advise talking with someone you trust about how to approach an older relative about a touchy subject, even to the point of practicing the situation by role-playing, with you and your friend taking turns playing the roles of yourself and your parent, and practicing handling tough responses from the parent. The calmer you are, the easier it will be for your parents to respond to the risky business of talking with their children—which might, after all, be a good name for another version of this book.

WHAT HAPPENS NEXT

The next two chapters, "Understanding Your Family and Older Relatives" and "Communication Styles," give you some useful ways of understanding families, aging, and communication. These chapters are then followed by three chapters focusing on the nuts and bolts of communicating with your parents: "Communication Skills," "Communication Strategies," and "Roadblocks and How to Overcome Them."

The remainder of the book focuses on a series of issues facing older persons and their families (housing, social matters, legal and financial concerns, health and well-being, confusion, death and dying, nursing homes, family matters, and you). Along with background information on each topic, ideas are presented as to how older persons might react to these situations as well as how you might react to their concerns. Some areas to consider before discussing each topic are presented, as well as some scenarios and relevant case histories. Finally, at the ends of chapters, additional resources are listed that may be of help if you choose to pursue the topic with your parents.

I hope that you benefit from the information and issues I raise. Putting this book together has forced me to think through how I communicate with my older relatives, when I communicate with them, and how much I listen to what they have to say. I have found a wealth of information and value from the people who have given me their family stories to use (disguising their identities, of course) as examples. It has been said that a conscientious teacher learns while teaching. I have found the same to be true in writing this book. I bid you well on your inquiry into communicating and talking with your parents.

2

Understanding Your Family and Older Relatives

A woman named Melanie, in talking with me about her mother's health condition, made the following observations.

> We have been a family that seemed distant but always pulled together in times of crisis. Although we had wanted to offer help to Mom when she started to have falls, it seemed as though she had to ask for help in order for it to work. When she finally went into the hospital, it was as if each of us knew what to do. I was in charge, but my brother had to okay the choice of nursing homes. I could never figure out whether Mom was stubborn, only acted that way around me, or was just old. She was nice to everyone else, but heaven forbid a family member should suggest that she keep the telephone near her bed. Are all families like this?

Melanie, in thinking about her mother and family, was addressing some central concerns and issues about families and aging. Families do act in ways that are consistent, even if they are not obvious to family members. Older parents interact differently with their children than with other people; certain "rules" and communication processes seem to emerge in particular families. In addition, there is the question of to what degree your parents' behavior is a function of their age.

This chapter looks at these issues, some basic ideas about families, and some reconsideration about "myths" about the elderly.

UNDERSTANDING YOUR FAMILY

What Is a Family?

A family is many things. It is a combination of people such as your mother and father and your grandparents, who grew up in their own families. It has "members" (not all of whom live together), level of income, ethnic background, religious persuasion, and males and females in assigned roles, be they father, mother, sister, brother, aunt, or uncle.

A family can include nonblood relatives (such as godparents and aunts or uncles by marriage). It may even include nonrelatives who function as family members, sharing in the bonds, roles, and functioning of the family unit.

A family can also be defined by its functions; including child rearing, learning social values, celebrating holidays, and observing major events such as births, weddings, and deaths. Some families might perform these functions differently than others, and some might do some of these things "better" than others, that is, with less stress and interruption of the family's routine or usual ways of living on a day-to-day basis.

Perhaps most important for our consideration is the idea that the family has *dynamics*, or systematic patterns of behavior and communication that affect how it operates. Think of your own family for a moment. How are decisions made? How are family problems identified and resolved? Who is usually a "leader" or a "follower"? How do you celebrate special events such as holidays? Also, how does everyone find things out about each other? Are your family members very tied to each other, do they operate quite independently of each other, or are they somewhere in between?

There are many theories about how families interact. Most of these accept the notion that the family is a "system." A family system has certain characteristics:

1. The interaction and functioning of the people in the family is greater than the individuals involved. Put another way, the whole is greater than the sum of the parts.

2. In order to understand any individual's functioning, one must appreciate how everyone else is involved. For our purposes, we have to appreciate that when we talk to our older relatives, our communication and the outcomes of our discussions affect us *and* other members of the family as well.

3. Each person's response is in turn the trigger (stimulus) for others to respond. The belief that one person caused something to happen oversimplifies a complex situation, in which the causes are frequently responses to something else, whether it's another person's behavior or some imagined incident.

4. Each person's view of the family will differ from others' views. In a sense, the family you grew up in was quite different from the family your brothers, sisters, and parents experienced. These differences can

show up in differing expectations and reactions to others and may need careful attention to create clear understanding about your purposes in talking with your parents.

5. The best (and perhaps the only) way to change one individual in a family is to make sure all other individuals are changing as well. Otherwise, the family will act in subtle ways to move the changed person back to what he or she was. This process can be called the family system's desire for homeostasis. Put another way, if we were going to make a change in how our parents listen to us, we would also have to think about how *we* talked with them. In addition, we would have to consider the implications of the changes for our brothers and sisters and perhaps include them in the process. Otherwise, they might inadvertently block the changes we are trying to make.

Family Norms, Values, and Rules

There are several aspects of family functioning that have strong implications for how we talk with our parents. One such aspect is *family norms*, or ways the family acts and interacts. Family norms refer to the actual behavior, words, and reactions of family members, rather than "what they think they should do." What a family "thinks it should do" is a different set of concepts, called *family values*.

An example may help to clarify the difference between a value and a norm:

> Lillian, age 79, was the mother of two children, Beth and George. Both Beth and George felt strongly that they should care for their mother (a value), but at the same time, as in the case of Melanie and her mother in the beginning of the chapter, they believed that help should be offered only when asked for (a norm). So, even though Lillian seemed to need help with shopping, Beth and George felt they had to wait until their mother told them she needed a ride to the store.

In this case, a value (caring for a relative) could not be acted on when it was felt by Beth and George because of a norm (help should be given only when requested). Values and norms can exist in harmony, but they can also be "in conflict."

A concept closely related to norms and values is that of family "rules," frequently unrecognized but potent guidelines for "appropriate" or "inappropriate" behavior. Some families, for example, have a rule that says

"Do not tell anyone you are angry" or "You may not show anger in any form." Other families have rules like "Do not tell people how much you like them" or "Do not encourage anyone too much." Other rules are less forbidding, like "Use good manners at the table" or "Give Grandma two days' notice before visiting" or even "Include Grandpa and Grandma in every family dinner."

Families have different sets of rules about different types of events. For example, in some families, there is open discussion about vacations and yet only one person makes decisions about financial matters.

Discovering Your Family's Norms, Values, and Rules. As an initial step in talking with your parents, it might make sense for you to take a little time to discover some of your family's norms, values, and rules. You can do this by first writing down what your family actually *does* regarding care of the elderly. Do they participate? How? Is there visiting, helping with chores, talking on the telephone? Who talks with whom about the important issues? These behaviors are your family's *norms* about care of the aged.

Next are the *values* or beliefs that exist in your family around care of the elderly. Think carefully about the ideas your family members would agree are important in caring for the elderly, and write them down. One hint is to include the sense of responsibility and caring that may derive from your family's cultural or religious background.

Now write down some of the *other* important values that operate in your family aside from those focusing on care of the aged. Remember, we are just at the value level, those things we give lip service to or believe deeply, even if we do not follow through on them. Examples of other values are "Take time for yourself," "Be true to your spouse," "Spend time with your children," or "It is important to have a job."

As you do this exercise, you might find yourself discovering that some of these values are in conflict when translated into action. You can find yourself pulled in two directions—toward your own values and toward those of your parents. You might find yourself torn between your spouse and your parents, or even between your children and your parents. These pulls are understandable, but if you leave them unresolved, they can only lead to stress or a burden on you, a situation that is not good for you, your parents or the others in your family.

Some experts in the field of family therapy—which seeks to treat all members of a family or at least to include family systems concerns in treating the relevant family members—think that conflicts between loyalties are the primary cause of distress in family members. Some sorting out of these loyalties becomes important if they cause you distress in caring for your parents.

Now, as a third step, think about your family's *rules* about the care of older relatives. What are you allowed to talk about? When? What are the norms and rules about making decisions? Who makes them? With input from whom? As you think about your rules, write them down on a separate list.

Also think about the impact of these rules on the family, including your older relative. How happy is everyone not only with decisions that are made but with the "process" of decisions or communication or problem solving? Do you have different rules for "difficult" decisions or issues than for easy ones—say, the difference between deciding whether to institutionalize an older relative or deciding when to have a family celebration of an eighty-fifth birthday?

A fourth step is to examine how your family's values, rules, and norms affect communication. Take a sheet of paper and make three columns on it. Write "Helps Communication" at the top of column 1, "Doesn't Affect Communication" at the top of column 2, and "Hinders Communication" at the top of column 3. Under each heading, list as many family rules, values, and norms from your other lists as you can. (Some items may actually be listed in two categories, because at times they may help communication and at other times hinder it).

As you do this, pay attention to any emotional reactions you have to the rules, values, and norms—any tension in your body such as a clenched jaw, tight facial muscles, or even an upset stomach. These reactions are signs of areas or issues around which you (and your older relative) are likely to feel tension.

Finally, look at your list. Consider *how* each norm, value, or rule could be handled differently to improve communication, understanding, and your parent's situation. This list and your ideas about what you would like to have changed can become one of the areas to consider talking about with your parents as well as the rest of the family.

Obligations, Roles, and Cultural Traditions

Sociologists have given us invaluable insights into family structure, ethnic groups, and traditional roles in thinking about families. Although the focus of this book is more on the psychological aspects of talking with your parents, any such discussion has to be done within the framework of the obligations, roles, and traditions that are part of your family's background and normative behavior.

Virtually every cultural group has its own traditions about who does what; how mothers, fathers, children, and occasionally grandparents, aunts, and uncles are supposed to act toward each other; and who is supposed to take care of specific family members when they are in need of help. When the aged need help, it is usually a spouse who takes care, followed by a daughter, daughter-in-law, and then son. (Of course, your individual family's situation may vary.)

Families also have culturally dependent obligations, such as providing the children with a trade or with a college education, belonging to a particular faith or denomination, or celebrating certain holidays as a family unit. One of the tensions between generations in several cultural groups in the United States today is that the cultural traditions are held to more strongly by the older generation than the "sandwich" generation—middle-aged persons who are both raising children and trying to be responsive to the needs of their elders.

> Jules was the devoted son of Carmen, his widowed mother who had made an independent life for herself through the neighborhood senior citizen center. Carmen, however, always felt bad that Jules did not visit her every weekend as people had done in the old country; instead, he would spend more time with his own wife and children. While she knew that things were different from the time when she was a girl in her country, she suffered silently, although it bothered her that her son did not give her the treatment she felt she deserved.

In this situation, Carmen felt that a cultural norm (visiting) was being violated by her son, but she also had a rule that she could not ask for what she wanted. The result was an understandable sense of discomfort. Inasmuch as cultural norms are part of your parents' identity, they may be hard to change. At the same time, only with some appreciation of both your own needs and the traditions or values held by your parents can you begin to discuss these generational differences and work toward their resolution.

This is not to say you have to give up your ideas or make your parents give up theirs; rather, it is that some of the disagreements or difficult issues arise not from stubbornness but from a life-style or an acceptance of behaviors that are part of a cultural tradition. On the other hand, traditions *can* change. Many traditions have had to adapt to new situations. The process of changing traditions in your own family may take time and effort on everyone's part. Understanding the importance of the tradition underlying your parents' difficulties in accepting change is an important part in helping them make needed changes.

Reciprocity and Exchange

A sense of exchange means that both parties in an interaction have a sense of give and take, that each person is getting as well as giving. When the relationship is one-way (or is perceived to be one-way by at least one person), there is likely to be tension and some movement out of the relationship. In a similar fashion, most people like to feel that there is reciprocity in relationships, that they are contributing as well as receiving benefit, aid, or emotional support.

Frequently, older persons do contribute to their family members in the form of gifts, child care, financial support, or advice. However, when they are faced with a difficult situation, such as illness, the death of a spouse, or a move to a new living situation, the family is called upon to provide counseling, support, or even financial assistance, often without there being a sense of exchange or reciprocity in the interaction.

Turning to the family, although it is the first line of defense for the elderly, may also be a source of ambivalence for them. It may be rationalized by thoughts such as "I took care of so and so when she was growing up, so it is all right for her to take care of me." I think the need for such justification comes from there being an inequality in terms of who is "giving" and who is "getting." Unfortunately, few people attempt to talk about it to lessen the guilt felt on both sides. Few people also attempt to make the exchange more even by utilizing the strengths and abilities of their parents even as they become more dependent upon others for support.

Parenting the Parent: a Myth in the Making

"Parenting the parent" (or "role reversal") is a term some experts use to describe shifts in relationships between parents and children as the parents age. It is a term that supposedly captures a change not only in what is "given" but in who does the giving and taking in the relationship.

Many adult children of the elderly find themselves becoming advisers, care providers, and sources of emotional and financial support to their parents. However, to *equate* these changes in the relationship with "parenting the parent" is misleading and potentially a problem in itself. (I think some of the problem lies in feeling, at some level, that if we are to be the parents of our parents, then we have to treat them as they treated us, *for better or for worse*.)

First of all, your parent is not a child, even if he or she exhibits "childlike" behavior. There is no evidence I know of that suggests that the mind of a sick or failing 80-year-old is the equivalent of that of a healthy three-year-old. Also, treating adults "like children" carries with it some incorrect assumptions about children, such as the beliefs that they need stern discipline, that they have to be spoken to in a patronizing way or in baby talk, and that they are likely to disobey and be uncooperative or otherwise difficult to manage.

Second, while you may be more nurturing or supportive to your parents now than you have been in the past, your purpose in providing care is not to "raise" them in the same manner that one raises children, but rather to help them cope and adapt to losses. We can nurture our parents; we can provide assistance at all levels, including the most basic tasks such as feeding and bathing. We may, in certain circumstances, need to set careful limits to protect our aging parents from harm in their homes. But we are *not* our parents' parents, nor are they our children.

Rosa, age 68, was dying of cancer. In the course of her illness and decline, which had been quite rapid, she had been transformed from a vital, active woman to the point where she needed help walking and bathing. She was also incontinent and wore adult diapers. I sat with her and her daughter, Kay. Kay began to talk about how their situation had "reversed," how now she was the "parent" and her mother was the "child." I watched Kay's discomfort play itself out on her face and body, and was also aware that Rosa was crying silently. Quelling my inclination to have them "talk things out" (an understandable therapeutic strategy), I said the following: "Kay, you are not her mother; she is not your child. Even if you are changing Rosa's diapers because she is incontinent, even if you are helping her walk, you are both adults. You can do all of these things and still be Rosa's adult daughter." I watched both of them relax as I spoke. Each, it appeared, was glad to be freed from the bind of having the daughter "parent the parent."

Tension (or stress or suffering or strain) is understood quite well by families. Tension refers to unpleasant feelings, anxiety, fear, concern, and/or anger between two or more family members. Frequently, when there is tension, there is decreased self-esteem for all parties. *Self-esteem* (or self-worth) refers to how you value yourself as a person, regardless of the feelings you are having at a particular moment.

Certain acts by others may be linked to how we feel about ourselves, such as having our spouse say "I love you," feeling "bad" when one of our children acts inappropriately, or feeling worthless if a superior criticizes our work. Similarly, our parents' self-esteem may be tied up in how they think we "should" act toward them, including "respecting" them as elders, keeping them out of a nursing home, or specific actions such as sending them a birthday card or making daily telephone calls.

Unfortunately, low self-esteem gets in the way of appreciating others' points of view when there are disagreements. It seems that disagreements, which are healthy and expected in part because no two people are exactly the same, frequently get turned into struggles over who is "right" or "wrong," "good" or "bad." When they do, self-esteem is really the issue, even though none of the people involved in a disagreement may have any desire to make the others feel bad about themselves.

At the same time, there is a time and place for disagreement and some tension in families. The tension that comes from disagreements is natural and expected. The tension that gets added on as a result of low self-esteem is both unhelpful and painful. I hope that after reading this book, when you have to talk with your parents about a potentially embarrassing, difficult, or otherwise emotionally charged issue, you will make every attempt to keep your sense of self-esteem out of the way (and out of harm's way), even though your parents may start to make "attacks" on it. Also respect the likelihood that your parents' self-esteem may get mixed up in the topic of discussion, since most of the ones I discuss in this book will be near and dear to them as well as to you.

Calibration. Calibration is a name given to the outcome of "fine-tuning" your reactions (and sense of self-worth) to the multitude of cues your parents give while communicating with you, as well as their "fine-tuning" their reactions to you when you are communicating with them. In some families, for example, a raised eyebrow means, "I am angry. You have hurt my feelings. I will not talk about it, and I am going to walk out of the room in the next minute." In other families, a certain tone of voice from one member means (to the others) that unless an apology is forthcoming, there will be a tirade in the near future.

Unfortunately, family members too frequently act as if they are correct in their interpretations of cues and, more important, they implicitly accept the "inevitable chain of events" associated with the cue. Then, understandably, they immediately begin to respond with their own cues and lowered sense of self-worth that actually furthers them on the "road to ruin." (Remember, each response is a stimulus for others, even if you do not mean it to be.)

Calibration cycles can be difficult to uncover. They are frequently not in the awareness of either party. At the same time, if you want to talk differently with your parent, one way to change things is to change how you react to "calibration" cues, which in turn can lead to your parents' changing their reaction to your reaction. (Chapter 6 gives you some suggestions in overcoming the roadblock of calibration responses.)

As you continue through this book, as you think about what you want to say to your parents and how to say it, remember that the background of your interactions with your parents is that you are members of the same family, with norms, values, rules, a cultural tradition, and patterns of communication. Appreciating these aspects can aid you in your quest for better communication.

UNDERSTANDING YOUR OLDER RELATIVES

Some readers might want to skip this section, saying, "I already understand my mother and father. After all, I've known them for a considerably longer period of time than this author has been alive." In some sense they are right—they do have a more complex understanding of the parent *from their own point of view* than I or anyone else could possibly have.

At the same time, I want to add some considerations to your existing picture of your parents, their likes, dislikes, strengths, weaknesses, hopes, wishes, fears, concerns, and activities. First, despite anyone's claims to the contrary, parents are not simply parents. They are people who themselves have been children, raised in a certain family set of norms and cultural traditions as well as in a specific setting in a specific period of history. They are also, or have been, brothers or sisters, nieces or nephews, aunts or uncles, workers and/or homemakers, and have had a variety of other roles and functions. Frequently, these are forgotten because when we are interacting with them, it is in the roles of parent and child.

There is a special set of bonds between children and parents that can be maintained with great strength throughout the life cycle. We can also hope, as adults, to have a greater appreciation of our own parents as people who have strengths, weaknesses, and the ability to misunderstand as well as the ability to change in positive ways. One way of putting it is that we need, as adults, to give "personhood" to our parents.

One important part of understanding your parents is being able to separate what you see, hear, or feel about them into three overlapping areas: that which is individual, that which is due to their being "old," and that which is part of the communication process with us. The individual parts of our parents have to do with their personalities, their likes and dislikes.

Too often, however, some of our reactions to our older relatives are based on inaccurate perceptions or expectations of what people their age do or how they should act. These perceptions can be called myths of aging. The attitude that promotes these myths or stereotypes is called agism, which is prejudicial against the elderly. I want next to review some of the more common myths and attempt to give you more accurate ways of thinking about behavior that might lead you to make incorrect conclusions about your parents. The third part, your interaction with your parents, is the focus of Chapters 3 through 6.

Myths and Truths about Aging

Senility. One of the most common misbeliefs about the elderly is that they are losing their minds, that memory loss is the first step in an automatic progression that leads to loss of bodily functioning, deterioration of thinking, and eventually death. A related belief is that all of us, if we live long enough, will lose our memory and judgment, and eventually forget where we are, who we are, and who our loved ones are. This belief leads to great fear among many of the elderly and their younger relatives as well, which in turn leads to a lack of discussion about any signs of memory loss because everyone fears that this is the first sign of senility.

Most elderly (over 80 percent) show *no* signs of impaired mental functioning associated with "senility." About half of those who do (and the signs are fairly specific) are suffering from a cause *other* than a deterioration of the brain found in conditions such as Alzheimer's disease. (Chapter 11 discusses the issues involved with confusion in the elderly in more depth.)

Although many older persons experience a degree of memory loss, it is usually minor and more of an inconvenience than anything else. It does *not* mean that an inevitable decline has begun. It also does *not* mean that nothing can be done about the memory loss. Simple aids like keeping lists of names and phone numbers, having a set place to put keys in the house, and writing down directions are useful tools to help older relatives, provided they can be suggested in ways that are not demeaning and provided that expected reactions like feeling foolish can be handled.

Memory loss is troublesome on a day-to-day basis. If family members believe the myth of senility (that all old people are losing their minds), it can also lead to older relatives being discounted in discussions or subtly being shunned by younger relatives.

> Paula, 92, had several health problems but seemed of sound mind, although she was a bit "forgetful." Over time, however, she began to ask her children to repeat information and would fail to recall many things she was told. Her children assumed that her problem was really one of memory loss and subtly let her know they were impatient with her "forgetfulness." Paula became withdrawn and hesitated to ask them any questions, preferring to nod her head as if she understood what they were saying rather than be the recipient of their "scorn" (which was actually frustration). It was only after a physician discovered her hearing loss and reassured the family that Paula had no severe mental impairment that they began to work out ways to make sure Paula understood what was being said to her.

Paula's situation has been repeated countless times. Families, not knowing what to do about a change in an older relative's functioning, assume it is due to "senility," become anxious, and avoid addressing the issue or give vent to mild recrimination, such as expression of impatience.

Incompetence. A related myth is that older people are incompetent, that they cannot really manage their affairs. In fact, nothing could be further from the truth. Most older adults manage their affairs quite well: about 90 percent take care of their bills, living arrangements, and daily activities quite independently. Older persons who need to have others manage their financial or living arrangements are a minority. Only 5 percent of the elderly, for example, live in nursing homes. Although about 86 percent of the aged have a chronic illness, less than half of all elderly have any physical limitation on their daily activities.

The reactions of others can make changes in physical functioning seem to be a sign of loss of competence for the elderly. The older person who moves slowly or needs a hearing or mobility aid may be judged as being incompetent in other areas of functioning and can, if given enough "guidance" by well-meaning but ill-advised relatives, begin to think of himself or herself as incompetent. One of the adages that best sums up research on ability and aging is "Use it or lose it." By acting toward older persons with physical limitations as if they are incompetent, we may well be sending them down a path they do not deserve or need to be on.

Rigidity. The myth of rigidity holds that as people become older, they become more rigid and set in their ways. There is little evidence of this notion in any research on aging that psychologists have done.

In fact, it could be argued that today's older people have gone through more changes in their lifetime than any other generation. Think for a moment about the changes brought by automobiles, airplanes, telephones, televisions, computers, and, on the social level, Social Security, Medicare, and issues like retirement. Older people have had to cope with more role changes and shifts in their status by virtue of age than younger people have had to. Most come through it fairly well.

If anything, psychological research has showed us that personalities are fairly consistent throughout the lifespan. The rigid old person is likely to have been a rigid young person. Put another way, the old crab was a young crab; the old willow tree that bends in the wind was a young willow tree as well.

At the same time, there are older persons who do not go along with suggestions others make to change their life-styles or living situations, even if such advice is warranted and may protect them from significant safety hazards. If this is the case, potential causes include individual personality type, particular psychological problems, *how* the suggestions are made, and fear.

Fear about what change may mean can be, if left unspoken or undiscussed, one of the greatest barriers to change in any age group. Fear does *not* mean that your parent cannot change or is rigid. It does mean that there are underlying concerns to be addressed by you and your parent before change will take place.

Emotional Fragility. There are many myths about emotions in old age, some of them claiming that old people are cranky, explosive, easily upset, or, conversely, passive, dependent, and unhappy. Actually, emotional style is consistent throughout the life cycle, one change perhaps being a heightened sense of turning inward in old age.

The problem with believing the emotional fragility myth is that expression of feelings by older persons can be downplayed or ignored.

Family members can be faced with social situations in which an older relative is forgetful, loud, or abrasive, or even needs to go to the bathroom at the "wrong" time. Their embarrassment, which is understandable, may give way to "explaining" the relative's behavior by phrases such as, "Well, he's old," or "She's a bit, you know . . . ," or other sentences that cover up embarrassment but do so at the cost of the older person's dignity.

There is no question that action may need to be taken in situations such as these, whether it is talking with the older relative, planning for the "emergency," or dealing with the insensitive stares and comments of other people. However, "excusing" the actions of older relatives *because of their age* is patronizing, inaccurate, and demeaning.

Sexlessness. Older people are stereotyped as being sexless and uninterested in sexual matters, and are the subjects of ridicule and scorn if they express themselves as sexual beings. These stereotypes take various forms, ranging from the "oversexed old lady" and the "dirty old man" to the old person who cannot have a sexual thought or, in case such an abnormal reaction does occur, cannot act on it. Older people are frequently treated as if gender differences are unimportant to them.

The truth is that many older people are quite able to have sexual reactions in both the general and specific meaning of the term. The biggest deterrent to sexual expression in old age is the lack of a suitable partner. In part, this is due to the high incidence of widowhood among older women.

Perhaps more important, older people need to be treated as if they are alive, with feelings, emotions, tenderness, and the ability to care. One way to discover (in a socially acceptable manner) the strength of sexually related issues for the elderly is to spend time talking to them about their lives. Ask in the course of discussion about their strong attachments to other people, including parents, spouses, and children. Pay attention to the strength of the bonds of affection and love that may be expressed. All of these are part and parcel of being human. Older persons are just as human as anyone else. As you prepare to go forth to talk about matters with your older parents, be prepared for them to be human. It will make your conversations go better and prepare you better for whatever may transpire between you.

In this chapter, I have tried to give you a quick tour of thinking about family functioning, family dynamics, and myths of aging as they may affect how you interact with your older parents. I have also alluded to some of the issues you may want to talk to your older relatives about. Before discussing these issues in some depth, however, I want to give you a framework for thinking about communication with your parents. Thus, the next four chapters focus on communication styles and skills, strategies that aid communication, and overcoming some roadblocks to communicating with aging parents.

RESOURCES

Butler, R. *Why Survive? Growing Old in America.* New York: Harper & Row, 1975. This book, one of the first popular books to explore aging, won the Pulitzer Prize. It is an excellent reference for many aspects of aging.

Satir, V. *Peoplemaking.* Palo Alto, Calif.: Science & Behavior Books, 1972. This book, which is cited at the end of several chapters, is one of the best and most readable books out about families, self-worth, and communication.

3
Communication Styles

Both David and Eve, the children of Cass, noticed that their mother had become somewhat reclusive in the past several years. They felt she should get out more and perhaps join a senior center.

When they approached the topic, David would become somewhat stern, pointing his finger in the air, and tell his mother she "should" go out. He would also explain all the reasons his mother should go out but not pay any attention to her side of the situation. After all, he thought, she looked sad. And besides, he knew a few other seniors who were happy at the senior center. So, of course, his mother would be happy there, right? Also, being seen with other people and seeing them should help her perspective on life. And if she was feeling sad, it was not his problem, because those feelings were more of a woman's concern.

Eve, on the other hand, became sympathetic when they talked with their mother, blaming herself for her mother's not going out, and found herself thinking that children should not let their parents get "this way." Eve sometimes felt that her mother did not have a problem, that it was hers instead, and that it was horrible that her mother was so unhappy. She did not feel that she should tell anyone how she felt, but rather made apologies for not helping out as much as she should.

Cass would respond to their suggestions by alternately disagreeing with anything David said and then quickly changing the topic and talking at length about her departed husband, how they used to talk together but now no one listened to her. She would also blame Eve for not giving her what she needed from her family. Cass would also argue with both of them for subsequent weeks, bringing up points they had made and telling them why their points were wrong.

David and Eve were frustrated about the situation and complained to their friends that their mother didn't hear a thing they said.

Both David and Eve, when asked why their mother was not going out, would answer to the effect that she would not change or that her mind was set. Neither realized that, in addition to their mother's communication style, their own behavior and communication styles were in part hindering their mother from understanding their care and concern and considering possible changes in her life-style.

There is an old saying that has great truth for this chapter: it isn't what you say, it's how you say it. Your personal communication style is unique. It covers everything that is communicated except for the specific meaning of the words you are using. Thus, *body language* (how you are standing, your gestures, your facial and bodily expression, your skin tone), *auditory aspects of your speech* (volume, pitch, tone, accent, inflection, pace of speech), *feelings* (such as anger, anxiety, love, and disgust), and *thoughts* (including concern about how others value you and your sense of family rules about talking about the matter at hand) all interact to create your individual style or customary ways of communicating.

There are many ways to examine communication styles. The ones discussed here represent a series of overlapping dimensions that may shed light on how you come across to your parents and how they come across to you.

COMMUNICATION CHANNELS

Communication channels refer to our five major senses: seeing (visual channel), hearing (auditory channel), feeling (kinesthetic channel), smelling (olfactory channel), and taste (gustatory channel). Each channel has a physical aspect (such as looking, hearing, or touching) as well as more "cognitive" or integrative aspects (such as observing, listening, or having feelings or reactions). In addition, we frequently use language that reflects one channel (such as *see*, *look*, and *view* for visual words; *hear*, *listen*, and *talk* for auditory words; and *feel*, *touch*, and *grasp* for kinesthetic words). Finally, we can think in channels (such as making a picture in your mind, talking to yourself, or having a "gut feeling").

One important aspect of your communication style is which channels you are primarily using and which channels your parent uses. In the example above, David was very visual, *seeing* or paying attention to how his mother looked. Eve, on the other hand, was very kinesthetic, *feeling* bad or guilty. Cass, however, was auditory, talking about how no one listened to her. In part because there was little overlap of their channels, the three had communication problems.

Each channel has its place in our functioning. It is important to realize that your major channel may not be the major one of another person, who will then have a different "view" or "word" or "feeling" about things. If channels do not match well, then you need to figure out how to communicate in your parents' channels as well as, perhaps, teach them how to communicate in yours.

OTHER ASPECTS OF COMMUNICATION STYLE

Along with the ideas of communication channels, experts in psychology and communication have developed a range of aspects of communication styles to better understand how we communicate and come across to others. The following dimensions represent some of the better-known aspects of communication styles and processes. As you read them, use them as guides to assess how you may be coming across to your parents (and they to you) without either of you being aware of it.

Open and Closed Styles

An open communication style is characterized by being responsive to the information and viewpoints of others (leading to "two-way" communication). A closed style is characterized by having little ability to take in information and views from others (leading to "one-way" communication).

We all vary in our degree of being open or closed depending on the subject and with whom we are talking. Our degree of openness may be conveyed by body language (for instance, arms and legs crossed usually conveys a message of being closed), eye contact (avoiding eye contact is a good way to suggest you are not interested in the other person), or auditory aspects (sounding "mechanical," talking fast, and interrupting are good ways to seem closed). In the example at the beginning of this chapter, David was fairly closed to his mother, and Eve was open, although neither was particularly effective in convincing her to change.

Person or Task Orientation

Another way to characterize your communication style is the degree to which you focus on the matter at hand (the task) and the degree to which you focus on the emotional aspects of what is going on (the person). Some people are more comfortable with one of these aspects than the other. Their style of communicating may reflect this. In extreme cases, there may be an inability to deal with part of a situation, as feelings and facts both are a part of any life situation.

In the case of David and Eve, David was much more task-oriented and Eve was person-oriented in responding to their mother's situation. In our culture, men are traditionally taught to be task-oriented and women person-oriented. However, there is clearly room for each of us to develop and attend to both qualities in talking with our parents.

Self-Disclosure

Self-disclosure represents your ability to talk about personal issues with others. People vary in the degree to which they feel comfortable self-disclosing. Some will disclose very little. Some will disclose everything that happens to them in such great detail that it wears on others. Some are more moderate. Both David and Eve, for example, while talking about important matters, would not share their feelings and reactions. Thus neither was particularly self-disclosing, which would hardly encourage their mother to talk directly with them.

It may be important for you to examine your ability to self-disclose about specific concerns you have with your parents. To what degree are you willing to risk their approval, rejection, or misunderstanding when you tell them what you really feel is important for them or how you really feel about something from the past?

Another aspect of self-disclosure is our comfort when others disclose personal information or feelings to us. Your subtle reactions to these feelings (including body stance, eye contact, and facial expression) may encourage or discourage your parents from talking about their feelings and reactions, even if you are spending time with them for the express purpose of "listening."

Acceptance

Acceptance implies that you can hear what is said without immediately judging the other person as being "good" or "bad." It does not mean you have to agree with what is said or that you never get angry or upset with another person. However, the ability to hear someone else's point of view (even if you know it is wrong or distorted) without becoming defensive is critical in talking with your parents. In the case of David and Eve, neither was "accepting" of their mother's behavior, although the form that nonacceptance took was quite different for each of them.

Unfortunately, the times we need to be most accepting are exactly those when it is most difficult to do so. It can be hard to feel accepting when your mother or father starts to become "parental" to make a point about you that has nothing to do with the matter at hand. Being accepting at those times requires both the realization that what you are hearing is more a matter of communication style than an attack on you, and a matter of faith that your parents are actually trying to fend for themselves, deal with stress, and make sense out of the world.

Along with accepting others, we also need to accept ourselves. Many of us carry around a part of our personalities that tells us to be perfect and never make mistakes, and if we do, that part punishes us, frequently more than the actual magnitude of the mistake warrants. One useful task to work on in preparation for talking with your parents is becoming more accepting of yourself as a person who has made mistakes, who has miscommunicated upon occasion, and who may not do everything perfectly the first or second or even third time.

Defensiveness

There are two overlapping meanings of the term *defensiveness*. The first is the most commonly understood one, used when someone is hostile or aggressive, "on the defensive."

The second definition means that an individual is using one of several unsuccessful ways to cope with anxiety or a feeling that his or her sense of self-esteem is being attacked. Several of the more frequently encountered defensive responses are *denial*, when an individual disclaims his or her feelings or behavior, as when Eve thought that her mother did not have a problem; *projection*, when the individual's inner problems are placed on everyone else except himself or herself, as when Cass put responsibility for her problems on Eve; and *rationalization*, making up logical-sounding excuses to cover one's own behavior, such as David's excuses for only paying attention to his mother's need for socialization.

Cognitive Errors

Another way of considering defensive reactions is to look at them as cognitive errors, which distort reality and subsequent reactions and behavior. Some of the most common cognitive errors are the following.

Magnification ("awfulization") is the process by which negative experiences come to seem worse than they are. Eve, for instance, made things out to be awful when in fact they were not so bad.

Overgeneralization is the process by which one event becomes "the truth" for all time. David overgeneralized other older persons' satisfaction with the senior center to conclude that his mother *would* be happy there.

Personalization is the process by which you may take statements by others to be statements *about you* when they are not. Eve personalized her mother's blame in the case above.

Arbitrary inference is the process by which incorrect or contradictory conclusions are drawn from facts. When David and Eve complained that their mother did not hear a thing they said, they were making arbitrary inferences. If anything, she heard quite well what they were saying.

Selective abstraction is the process by which one focuses on only one aspect of a problem, ignoring the full context in which it takes place. Eve and David focused on their mother's isolation and need for participating in a senior center, perhaps excluding possible health problems or other options for helping her cope as a single older woman.

In addition, some of our family rules are based on cognitive errors or "irrational beliefs," characterized by an overreliance on "shoulds" (e.g. the belief that we should be perfect in everything), magnification of the negative side of a situation, and a sense that one cannot rely on oneself to solve problems and handle difficult situations. To the degree you have these types of belief, you will have difficulty talking with your parents.

Albert Ellis, Aaron Beck, and David Burns are three authors who have written extensively on overcoming irrational beliefs and cognitive errors in daily living. Their works (some of which are listed at the end of this chapter) represent one way of changing these aspects of your communication style.

COMMUNICATION STYLES: SATIR'S CATEGORIES

Defensive Communication Styles

One of the best systems for understanding how defensiveness and communication style interact is the work of Virginia Satir. Her book *Peoplemaking* (1972) is one of the recommended readings for anyone who wants more information about families, rules, and communication.

Satir has developed four types of defensive styles of communication. According to Satir, defensive styles are learned in the family and therefore can be relearned. Defensive communication takes place when we are under stress or somehow perceive what is going on to be a threat to our self-esteem. Think for a moment about the most difficult thing you have to talk about with your parent. Is there likely to be anything he or she may say that will be felt by you to be an attack on your sense of self-worth? In all probability, the answer is yes.

Consider the following examples of mother-daughter interactions.

BLAMING

Daughter: Mother, we have to talk.

Mother: Oh? What do we have to talk about?

Daughter: [becoming angry, tight, pointing her finger] Mother, you never listen to me. Why do I always bother to try to make things work with you, anyway?

PLACATING

Daughter: Mother, we have to talk.

Mother: Oh? What do we have to talk about?

Daughter: [conciliatory, feeling guilty] Well, I'm sure its all my fault that I haven't made it clear to you yet . . . I'm sorry I brought it up.

BEING SUPERREASONABLE

Daughter: Mother, we have to talk.

Mother: Oh? What do we have to talk about?

Daughter: [aloof, reasoning] I read in the newspaper that seventy percent of the time a daughter and mother try to communicate, there is a substantial chance of some interchange.

BEING IRRELEVANT

Daughter: Mother, we have to talk.

Mother: Oh? What do we have to talk about?

Daughter: [getting silly] You're such a card. Heard any good jokes lately?

BEING CONGRUENT

Daughter: Mother, we have to talk.

Mother: Oh? What do we have to talk about?

Daughter: [in touch with her feelings and with feeling self-esteem] Mom, I want us to spend the next few minutes on something important. It is hard for me to discuss this with you, but I want us to try. I am concerned about what has happened to you lately. . . .

Each of the first four interactions had the daughter responding to the mother's seemingly harmless inquiry with a defensive type of response. That is, in each case, the daughter felt that her self-esteem was somehow threatened, and her response was an attempt to keep self-esteem up and anxiety down. In addition, each of the first four responses had several other things in common. In each, there were several components that did not make sense together. That is, they were incongruent. In addition, in each of the first four, the daughter did not (and could not) talk about how she felt or how she felt about herself for having the feelings she had (another way of describing self-worth).

Although there are no hard and fast statistical figures on how frequently the first four defensive forms of communication are used, Satir has estimated that over 95 percent of the communication in this world is incongruent. In tense family situations, that figure is probably an understatement.

Why, you may ask, are we so defensive with our families? In part, we are victims of our family background. Defensive ways of handling stress have been with us for centuries. However, almost anyone would agree that defensive communication is not useful, that it leads to other problems, and no one really benefits from it. Clearly, then, it is to everyone's advantage to decrease defensive communication and increase nondefensive (or congruent) communication.

All defensive communication comes from an attempt to survive a threat. It is not a deliberate attempt to attack others. That awareness, along with learning how to avoid getting caught up in a defensive communication cycle with your parents, is among the most important ideas you can take away with you from this book. As a step in this direction, let us now take a closer look at the four defensive styles of parent–adult child communication illustrated above and then compare them to the fifth style, being congruent.

Blame. In the type of defensive style characterized as blaming, there is an attempt to make the other person the source of one's fears or threats to self-worth. Blaming is frequently characterized by phrases such as "It's *your* fault," "You *never* . . .", or "You *always*. . . ." The blamer is frequently in a mind-set of disagreeing with almost everything. Bodily reactions include tightness in the neck and arms, and there is frequently a good deal of finger pointing by the person doing the blaming. To the person being blamed, the blamer seems both powerful and controlling. In reality, the person doing the blaming is scared and uncertain. But, sadly, there is rarely the opportunity to discuss being scared or the fragile sense of self-worth, as the two most natural responses to blame—guilt and anger—rarely lead either party to talking about what is going on. In the original example at the beginning of this chapter, both David and Cass could become blaming at times, "arguing" with each other.

Placating. The defensive style called placating can be said to be the opposite of blaming. That is, placating phrases include "It's *my* fault," "I always . . . ," or "You're right, I never. . . ." The placater will go along with others, even if she or he disagrees, just to be sure no one else's feelings are hurt. The bodily sensations of placating include stooping down, humbling oneself, and, at times, signs of gastric distress ("nervous stomach"). Eve, who tended to be apologetic to her mother, was a placater.

Perhaps surprisingly to the placater, others respond to being placated by becoming angry. It is frustrating never to know what other people really believe as they go along with what they think we want to hear. Placaters can be considered manipulative, "saccharine sweet," or occasionally "martyrs," even though they themselves only feel they are trying to survive a threatening situation by pleasing others.

Being Superreasonable. The third form of defensive communication, being superreasonable, means using an intellectual or rational-sounding approach that is actually irrational. Superreasonable people seem to have all the facts under control and can intimidate others by their apparent storehouse of knowledge. They may use big words and a significant amount of references to what they read in the paper, in the encyclopedia, and in specialized magazines. The body of a person being superreasonable is rigid, with the eyes slightly defocused and looking out into the distance as the voice spouts the "fountain of knowledge." David, as you may recall, along with being blaming toward Cass, also displayed superreasonableness.

Others tend to tune out the superreasonable person after a while, in part because they cannot follow what he or she is saying. The person being superreasonable is also not terribly open to other information or views and may actually not hear what others are saying, not because of physical problems, but more because of a defensive communication style.

Irrelevance. Satir's fourth type of defensive communication, irrelevance, is the fine art of steering clear of any topic that is potentially threatening by distracting attention away to flights of fancy, humor, or another topic entirely. In the situation described at the beginning of this chapter, Cass's changing of the topic of discussion could be viewed as being defensive and irrelevant.

The body movements associated with irrelevance are disjointed, with arms and legs almost going in different directions. Others feel removed from the distracter (another name for the person being irrelevant) and cannot understand his or her behavior. But again, the person being irrelevant is trying desperately to survive, to increase self-worth, and is doing the best he or she can.

Congruent Communication

The first four styles of communicating all have certain things in common. First, each is an unsuccessful attempt to ward off anxiety or a sense of threat to self-esteem. Second, each brings out defensive reactions in others. Third, each does not give those who use it a good opportunity to discuss feelings or feelings about themselves (i.e., self-esteem). Fourth, each is learned and can therefore be unlearned or changed to more effective and healthy ways of communicating.

At the same time, one can view each of these defensive styles as containing the seeds of useful attributes if employed appropriately. Blaming, when transformed to include respect for others' feelings, may become the basis for being assertive. Placating, when transformed to include respect for one's own wishes and feelings, may become a true sense of caring. Superreasonableness, when transformed to include respect for feelings on both sides, can be one's use of intelligence. Irrelevance needs to include staying on the topic at hand, as well as some sense of one's own and others' feelings; then it can be transformed into creativity or the ability to make connections between facts, ideas, and people.

All of these, when transformed, have the qualities exemplified in the fifth communication example given at the beginning of this section. They are *congruent*. Congruent communication is quite different from defensive communication. Congruence means, in Satir's system, that the words, feelings, and body of the person communicating are consistent. That is, one can feel one's anger, love, or joy; one's body language reflects one's inner feelings; and the words, tone of voice, and other aspects of communication are consistent.

Being congruent does not mean that you have to say everything you believe or that you can't disagree or even shield how you feel from others. It does, however, mean that you make many more conscious choices about how you act on the way you feel and that you can comment about your feelings, self-worth, and what is going on between you and the other person. Being congruent is easier on one's mental health and is most likely to get your intended message across to others.

One of the issues that come up in discussions of these styles and how they relate to parents is anger. Anger is one of the feelings we have most difficulty with, in part because it is so frequently associated with blame and attacks on self-worth, not to mention physical attacks. Satir claims that anger is, in fact, a secondary emotion. If you think about it, anger is as much a "response" of tension and energy that needs to be discharged as a "feeling." Anger usually is a physical response to feeling hurt, disappointed, abandoned, or "put down."

Be that as it may, it is not uncommon for children (and parents) to feel anger for a variety of reasons. The only way I know to be congruent about anger is to talk about it. Given the fact that there is energy in anger that needs to be discharged, along with talking about it, there is also a need for venting it or getting it "off one's chest." The venting and the talking are not (and indeed should not be) done simultaneously. It is also possible to vent to others and *then* talk about the anger with your parents, the goal being to both decrease negative feelings and find ways of handling situations so that anger does not develop.

All of the aspects of your communication style go into what you say to your parents. I hope that this introductory discussion has given you some useful thoughts about where your own stumbling blocks are or insights into how you might come across without knowing it that, in turn, makes your discussions with your parents more difficult than they have to be. The next few chapters of this book get into some of the nitty-gritty of talking with your parents—specifically, skills, strategies, and roadblocks and some ways to overcome them.

RESOURCES

Bandler, R., J. Grinder, and V. Satir. *Changing with Families*. Palo Alto, Calif.: Science & Behavior Books, 1976. An excellent book that integrates the work of Satir and that of Bandler and Grinder on communication channels. It also looks at calibration cycles and how they affect families.

Beck, A. *Cognitive Therapy and the Emotional Disorders*. New York: New American Library, 1976. Focuses on the cognitive components of emotional problems and ways to work with emotional disturbances.

Burns, D. *Feeling Good: The New Mood Therapy*. New York: Signet Books, 1980. Focuses primarily on depression but has many good exercises to use in changing the cognitive components of how we feel. It is more for a nonprofessional audience than Beck's work.

Ellis, A., and R. A. Harper. *A Guide to Rational Living*. Hollywood: Wilshire Books, 1973. Outlines Ellis's "rational-emotive" approach to changing the thoughts that lead to destructive feelings and behavior.

Satir, V. *Peoplemaking*. Palo Alto, Calif.: Science & Behavior Books, 1972.

4
Communication Skills

Communication skills are specific methods of conveying your feelings, questions, and points of view that should, if used judiciously, create better understanding and relationships. They are best used, of course, if you are congruent and nondefensive. An incongruent style can easily override the benefits of any communication skill.

At times, individual issues about self-esteem or family norms are so strong that a well-intentioned effort may fall flat. So as you read about these skills, think about them and decide for yourself which (if any) might make your discussions with your parents go more smoothly, with better results for both of you.

SKILLS FOR INFORMATION EXCHANGE

Consider the following exchange between Brian, a middle-aged man, and his mother, Gina, who is in her seventies. Brian is concerned because his father has been in the hospital for surgery and is going home in two days for a one-month recuperation. Brian is trying to find out what his mother wants or needs the first day or so that his father will be home.

BRIAN: Mom, do you have enough food?
GINA: Of course I do, we went shopping the other day.
BRIAN: When you get low, can I take you shopping?
GINA: I'll call you.
BRIAN: Mom, should I come over the morning Dad comes home?
GINA: I don't know. I'll call you.
BRIAN: O.K. [He thinks she does not want any help and is being stubborn. But after a bit of silence, he begins to feel frustrated.] Mom, what kind of help can I give you? I need to know what you need.

At that point, Gina begins to tell him how unsure she is and that she would like him to give them the morning alone but be there in the afternoon.

This exchange, up to the point where Gina says, "I don't know," is a potential "disaster" in that Gina and Brian are not exchanging information effectively. This part of their conversation could have benefit if Brian had used more effective skills to find out what his mother needed. Two such skills that would have helped him are open-ended questions and paraphrasing.

Open Questions

In the example above, Brian asked questions that both limited his mother's "choices" in replying and were best answered by one- or two-word responses. This type of question is called a closed-ended question. It is likely that Gina, after hearing a few of these, would decide that her son is avoiding the "real issues" and may, without being aware of it, go along with him to "be polite." It was only when he asked a more open-ended question ("Mom, what kind of help can I give you?") that she could talk about what was on her mind.

Open-ended questions cannot be answered easily with one word. They encourage others to talk about what they are feeling, thinking, or remembering at that moment. They allow others to have some control over what they say, how they say it, and how much they say.

Open-ended questions, much like an open communication style, imply that both people in the discussion "control" the discussion. In some families, control is usually *not* shared, and there may be a period of distrust and uncertainty when you begin to use skills such as open-ended questions. It may feel risky to you to give up control in asking such questions and for your parents to respond to them. Also, some people do not want to know what their parents are thinking or feeling. However, if you do not ask, you have no one but yourself to hold accountable for your ignorance about your parents' wishes, fears, or concerns.

Paraphrasing

Paraphrasing is the fine art of repeating what the other person said in your own words. Paraphrasing is used to show that you are listening and to check whether you have understood what was said. If your parent has a tendency to ramble on in making decisions or in setting logistics—such as giving you a day and time to come over for dinner—paraphrasing may be quite important, as it allows you to play an active part in the discussion instead of passively nodding your head and then remembering later that you never understood when you were to come over.

Take a look at the sentences in the left-hand column below, and decide how you might paraphrase them in your own words. Some possible paraphrasings are given on the right. Compare them with yours.

PARENT	ADULT CHILD
Son, you have always been a good boy to me. Why are you trying to hurt me now?	You're saying that you feel that while I've always paid attention to your wishes, I'm not paying attention to them now.
Dear, you just don't understand. A woman my age just can't pick up and leave her home.	You're saying that I cannot understand that you are set against leaving your house because you feel you are too old.
My other children don't care for me.	Do you mean that you think the others do not care for you the way I do?

Notice closely that in each of these rather difficult situations, the child is not passing judgment or reacting to what is said, but rather is trying to understand what the parent is saying. This step is very important in communicating. One advantage of paraphrasing is that it allows you to focus on your parent and what he or she might be meaning rather than focusing solely on your reaction to what is said. As you may remember, one of the problems in parent-child communication is calibration, or slipping into potentially destructive communication cycles. Paraphrasing before going on to your own reactions is a good way to decrease your own calibration responses.

SKILLS FOCUSING ON EMOTIONAL SUPPORT

Kate, age 80, had been in the hospital for an infection. As she was getting ready to be discharged, her daughter, Carol, came by for her daily visit. Carol was concerned about her mother, but had responsibilities of a career and family. Also, they had not been close in the past. All of these factors made Carol fearful that her mother would make demands on her that she could not meet. Kate, on the other hand, wanted to be as independent as possible, but was still concerned about feeling abandoned by her family. Their discussion at the hospital went as follows:

KATE: Carol, you can only stay a short while with me here and then you have to go to work. Who will take care of me at home?
CAROL: [shaking her head, frowning slightly, then crossing her arms and moving back in her chair] Mom, there's nothing to worry about. I'll call you tonight.
KATE: I'm so weak.
CAROL: Yes, Mom. [After a few uncomfortable moments, Carol smiles, gives her mother a dutiful peck on the forehead, and leaves the room, looking at her watch to see if she will be late for work. Kate watches this, tears forming in her eyes, and decides she cannot count on her daughter for anything.]

Both Kate and Carol have unwittingly contributed to the hard feelings that exist between them in that neither talks directly about how she feels and what her concerns are. At the same time, Carol may be able to provide needed emotional support to her mother without becoming so drawn into her mother's situation that she would have to sacrifice career and family.

Verbal Reassurance

Verbal reassurance means that your words convey that you care about the person with whom you are talking, appreciate his or her feelings, and respect him or her as a human being. Being reassuring can let your parent know you are interested in talking about "private" or "personal" matters, that you are strong enough to hear some not-so-nice things, and that your parent has your permission or invitation to continue to talk about emotional issues that he or she has just started to discuss with you, perhaps for the first time.

One important issue in reassurance focuses on what we can realistically reassure an older person about. We certainly cannot guarantee a longer life, happiness, or good health. Is reassurance trying to be cheerful when things are not so?

The answer is an emphatic no. Reassurance that promises there is nothing to worry about when in fact there is something to worry about is false reassurance and will often come across as phony and incongruent, even with the best of intentions. (Carol, by saying, "There is nothing to worry about," is guilty of giving false reassurance.) At the same time, we can reassure our parents that we will listen to them, that we will be caring, and that we will respect them. Reassurance can be of great help even in the most difficult of circumstances, because it is often the fear of abandonment that makes difficult circumstances even more frightening for older persons.

Look at the statements in the left-hand column below. Then think of what you could say in similar circumstances that would be truthful and yet reassuring. Compare your responses with those in the right-hand column.

PARENT	ADULT CHILD
Son, you can only stay with me a short while and then you have to go home. Who will take care of me? [said in the hospital]	Mom, you're right that I have to go home. I know you're worried, and I would be too if I were in the hospital. Do you want me to call tonight? Or I can call from work.

Note in this case that the son decides that some extra contact might be needed and checks it out with his mother. Compare this with Carol's response to Kate.

I have to go to the nursing home, I know. But I'm so scared that I'll become just like some of the people there.	It is scary to go to a nursing home. I'll be staying in close contact with you, especially in the beginning, to be sure that you get the best care and that there are things for you to do.

In this case, a promise is being made not to abandon the older person as well as to watch out for his or her welfare. A promise made should be a promise kept.

I lost my keys and I can't remember my new doctor's name. What's happening to me?	Mom, I don't know what your memory loss means. I'll work with you to find out if it's major or minor and if something can be done about it.

Each of the above examples begins to illuminate the types of emotionally laden issues we are faced with in talking with our parents. Each is discussed in more depth in the following chapters, but even here, I hope you can see how reassurance can have benefit and keep the lines of communication open at a time when you and your parent may need it most desperately.

Nonverbal Reassurance

Along with giving words of comfort, there are ways of adding to these expressions with your body, face, and voice. Some of the more commonly understood ways include nodding your head along with vocalizations like "Um-hmm"; maintaining eye contact; and keeping an "open" body position—not with arms folded or moving away, as in Carol's case, but letting your body express the message "I am here to accept you, not reject you."

Silence

One of the most underrated forms of effective communication is knowing when to sit quietly without saying a word. In counseling sessions, such silent moments frequently occur when the client is deep into her or his thoughts and feelings. The same can hold true in talking with your parents. Many of the most precious moments can be shared in silence, as long as it is not the awkward silence that makes each person feel that he or she needs to say something to make it go away, which was the case for Carol and Kate.

Empathy

Empathy refers to showing another person that you appreciate his or her feelings and, to some degree, feel the same things. Empathy is quite different from sympathy or pity, which carry with them a subtle judgment of the other person. Empathy implies acceptance, but at the same time does not carry with it the sense that the listener is overwhelmed by the feelings of the other person.

Empathy can be shown in words, in expressions, in touch, and in deed. (Note that Carol did not convey much empathy with her touch, which was a "peck" on the forehead.) In part, its form will depend on you, your parent, and your cultural and family norms and history. Empathy is what I use to describe the meaning of what is sometimes conveyed when a parent says, with love and admiration, "My child really understands me."

The relationship between Kate and Carol deserves one last comment. It is understandable that Carol did not "give" more support to Kate, because she feared that any support she gave might lead to increasing demands from her mother. The fear of being overwhelmed by both emotional and time demands is real for many children of the elderly. However, it is also possible to have limits on involvement and give full emotional support, knowing that you do not have to solve all the problems but recognizing that at times, what your parent needs is a listening ear.

SKILLS FOCUSING ON SHARING FEELINGS

Joan's husband, Rick, had died. Their daughter, Rachel, felt after several weeks that Joan should get over the death and get on with her life. She did not know how to tell her mother this and instead offered to take her mother out to meetings, to organizations, or even for lunch, all of which her mother refused. They spent little time talking about Rick, in part because Rachel thought she would do her mother harm by "dwelling" on his death. What Rachel would say when the topic came up was, "Mom, you should get over this."

This situation, like many others facing family members of the elderly, is one in which there are needs on both sides to talk about feelings. While family norms, history, and communication patterns all influence how we discuss feelings, there are several skills that can aid us in sharing feelings with our parents. They include the use of "I" statements, reflection, the use of touch, and active listening.

"I" Statements

"I" statements represent a way of taking responsibility for your own feelings and perceptions. This is frequently done by using the word *I* as the first thing to come out of your mouth when you are discussing feelings. By doing so, you are being honest, ascribing emotion and reasons where they belong, that is, to yourself. In Satir's system, discussed in the preceding chapter, the word *I* can be used to decrease blame (it stops the infamous "you" statement), and it can be used to decrease placating (when used to acknowledge that you have feelings and rights). In the relationship between Rachel and Joan, Rachel used a "you" statement ("You should get over this"). She might have done better to talk about her own feelings and wishes, rather than putting them on her mother. For example, she could have said, "Mom, I think you can put this behind you."

Think about how the statements on the left below could be transformed into "I" statements. Some possible transformations are included in the right-hand column.

You don't love me.	I feel no love from you.
You're right.	I think you are right.
This is the way it's going to be.	I need us to do it my way.
You made me love you.	I loved you.
Mother, you have to decide!	Mother, I want you to decide.
This is silly.	I feel this is silly.

Although the meaning of both sentences in each pair is roughly the same, the statements on the right side, as negative as some are, are likely to be better understood than the ones on the left, which will come across as damning, overgeneralized, and authoritarian.

Reflection

Reflection is the art of focusing on the feelings in another person's words and giving them back in your own words. Much like paraphrasing, it serves to tell the other that you are trying to understand him or her and can serve as a brake on overreacting to what is being said.

Reflection also tends to deepen any emotional state being experienced. It may be a bit scary to think about using reflection with your parents. People like Rachel may think that "dwelling" on negative feelings is unhealthy. Indeed, if all we did was focus on negative feelings, not much else would happen. However, by reflecting feelings back, we are also indicating that our parents are not "alone," which in turn can help lift a sense of despair. At the same time, you should not feel obliged to use reflection at all times. I would rather have you consider it one way to be close with your parent and to help both of you deal with hard feelings, but not the only way.

Look at the statements below on the left side of the page that could be made by an older parent. Then examine the "reflective" response that could be made by an adult child on the right side of the page to see how reflection could be used to help the parent understand and sort out his or her feelings.

PARENT	REFLECTION BY ADULT CHILD
I'm so alone since your father died.	You miss him.
Why don't you visit me like you should?	You're angry with me.
I will never get over this stroke.	You must feel helpless and hopeless.
It takes one parent to raise four children, but four children can't take care of one parent.	You feel abandoned by us.

Touch

All families have rules and norms about touch, including when to touch, where to touch, and even what touch means. In some families, not touching means you are angry. In others, touching only briefly can mean the same thing. And in other families, a brief touch can mean that everything is just fine. As a culture, we are fairly unsophisticated about using touch to convey care. Men historically have had strong rules against touching other men, even their fathers, although this seems to be changing. Women have had more latitude, but even so, there still exist strong rules and feelings about whom to touch and when and how to touch them.

At the same time, touch plays an important role in our communication with anyone, including our parents. Think for a moment how you could, if you wished, convey fear, excitement, hope, or care through holding your parent's hand. Touch can be used to give reassurance, to show that you are paying attention to another person, as well as to express affection and concern. Its value should not be understated in thinking about how to talk with your parents.

As with the other skills mentioned in this section, touch can be misused or used unwisely if you force it, are defensive in its use, or even feel uncomfortable with it, all of which could lead to an incongruent touch message. Some people do not like to touch or be touched. Although this can be altered with practice, it may take time to change your (and your parent's) patterns of when and how to touch. So, as in the case of other suggestions for better communication, you have to be the best judge of how and when to use touch with your parents.

Active Listening

All of the skills mentioned above can be used to "actively listen" to your parent. When you are actively listening, you have a sense of acceptance about the other person; you try to understand both the feelings and the content of what is being said; you are empathic and appreciative; and you respect the other person. At the same time, you maintain your own sense of identity and the freedom to agree and disagree with what is being said. These aspects are at times difficult to maintain in balance, but they are a useful goal for which to strive.

SKILLS FOR CONFRONTATION

Stephanie was the 36-year-old daughter of Marilyn, age 63. Marilyn, who had always been a bit domineering, insisted on taking her daughter shopping at least once a month. Stephanie did not enjoy the trips, as her mother would use them to complain about Stephanie's husband, their children, and the rest of the family. She also found that the trips took three to four hours out of a busy weekend. Ideally she wanted to make the conversation go differently, shop during the week, and make the shopping trips shorter, but she did not know how to talk about the situation.

At her wit's end, Stephanie decided that she had better talk about changing the day they went shopping first and discuss her mother's criticisms of the children later on. "Mother," she said one day while they were together, "I want to make a change in our shopping arrangements. The situation is really difficult for me on the weekends. I would like to go shopping with you for a few hours during the week."

"Well", her mother replied, "if you feel that way . . ."

"No, Mother, I don't feel 'that way.' I need to have the weekends freed up for the children. I would like to go with you on Tuesday instead of Saturday."

"You're just saying that because you know how much it hurts me. If you took proper care of your family, then they wouldn't be the way they are, if you ask me."

"Mom, we are also going to have to talk about how you talk about my family. I want to do it soon and get some things straightened out. However, first things first. I still intend to go out with you, but it has to be Tuesday."

It took more than this one conversation for both Stephanie and Marilyn to get used to the changes Stephanie was requesting. Marilyn would challenge her daughter, "forget" that the day had changed, and continue to make comments about the family when the two of them were shopping. Stephanie also needed more than one conversation to request that her mother stop downgrading other family members. However, Stephanie was eventually able to get her mother to decrease her "guilt induction" and negative statements about the family by confronting her when they came up.

Confrontation refers to a group of skills that focus on how you set limits, handle disagreements, and deal with uncomfortable feelings and perceptions about your parents. Confrontation does *not* mean blowing your top or being hostile. In the example above, Stephanie was strong, firm, and direct, but at the same time she followed several of what I think are useful ways of dealing with a confrontation in that they led to a solution that worked for her and (albeit slowly) for her mother. The types of skills Stephanie used included meta-commenting, saying no, positive disagreement, and assertion.

Meta-commenting

Meta-comments are statements about the interaction you are having that describe how you see the relationship between you and your parents and how you feel about it. In the situation above, Stephanie explicitly stated that she needed to talk with her mother about shopping and that she was not happy with how things were working out. Each of these was a meta-comment, a comment about the situation. Meta-comments are useful in that they let your parents know where you stand on issues and can set the stage for them to tell you how they feel and what is behind some of their words and behavior.

Saying No

No is a word with a range of implied and perceived meanings that may have nothing to do with the matter at hand. *No* can mean "I have power and you have none"; it can mean "I do not love you"; it can mean "I am angry with you" or even "You have no value." *No* can also mean that what you are asking is not what I can do, or that I am telling you my choice about a decision. The ability to give a firm yet nonblaming no is imperative in confrontation with parents, since the first group of connotations may well run through your history together. It is an integral part of positive disagreement and being assertive, which are described briefly below.

Positive Disagreement

In many families, disagreement is tantamount to saying "I do not love you." Stephanie avoided this trap by using positive disagreement; that is, she stuck to the point of disagreement (what day to go shopping) and separated the implied issues of self-worth ("If you feel that way . . .") from the issue at hand. In so doing, she gave the message that she and her mother could feel positive about each other, yet still disagree.

Assertiveness

Assertiveness has been defined as the ability to make your needs and wishes known to others while respecting their rights. It is frequently differentiated from aggression (blame), which violates the rights of others, and passivity (placating), which violates your own rights. In the example above, Stephanie was assertive in stating that she needed a change in shopping dates and in continuing to make this known even when Marilyn resisted the change. Stephanie did not lose her temper when her mother attempted to keep the shopping expedition at its previous time, but was firm, specific, and stood her ground without being hostile.

Types of Assertiveness. There are several types of assertiveness, including saying no to unreasonable requests, asking for what you need, requesting others to stop offensive actions, saying yes to others, and even accepting a compliment. You may find that you do better in some of these types, while in others you may need improvement to give you a better sense of control over your confrontations with your parents.

Aspects of Assertiveness. Along with having a focus (such as saying no), an assertive response needs to be congruent; that is, your body language, phrasing, voice tone, eye contact, and intonation should all be consistent with the message you are getting across and should not include aspects of hostility or passivity. Each aspect of assertiveness can be practiced. Feel free to use a mirror or ask for a friend's help to find out if any aspects of your assertive statements give mixed messages.

Developing an Assertive Response. There are several useful steps you can consider following to develop assertive responses to use with your parents.

1. Analyze the situation. Is it one in which it is appropriate for you to be assertive?
2. Determine what the content of your message should be. What do you want or need to say?
3. Practice saying the message to yourself. As you imagine the situation, work on being as relaxed and "strong" as possible.
4. Practice saying the message to someone other than your parent. Have the person tell you whether you are convincing and what aspects of your message are not convincing or assertive.
5. Practice having another person give you "curve balls" or challenges that try to get you to back off your assertive position. Develop counterattacks (e.g., "Yes, and I want . . . ," or "Let's talk about that later") that are assertive and also allow you to continue to make your point.
6. When you are ready, give your message to your parent.
7. After you have done it, evaluate how it went. If things did not work out well, determine what (if anything) you could do differently the next time to be assertive, to have your opinions and needs appreciated, while appreciating those of your parents.

Confrontation skills, much like the other skills in this chapter, should result in better talks and interaction with your parents as long as they are done in the spirit of trying to make things work. At the same time, the situations facing many families require considerable thought about how to approach topics, what to say, and when to use certain skills. The next two chapters will provide you with further ideas on how to talk with your parents.

RESOURCES

Alberti, R. H., and N. L. Emmons. *Your Perfect Right*, 4th ed. San Luis Obispo, Calif.: Impact Books, 1982. One of the original books about assertion. It has many of the major points to be made about being assertive.

Bach, G. R., and L. Torbet. *The Inner Enemy*. New York: Berkeley Books, 1985. One of several books by Dr. Bach about positive uses of aggression. Useful background in handling confrontation.

Gordon, T. *Parent Effectiveness Training*. New York: Peter Wyden, 1970. This book, along with the others in the Effectiveness Training series, has basic and useful information about active listening and communication.

Rogers, C. R. *Carl Rogers on Personal Power*. New York: Delacorte Press, 1977. One of many books by the person most identified with client-centered therapy, which focuses on empathy and unconditional positive regard for others.

5
Communication Strategies

A communication strategy is a preplanned approach to handling a specific problem or topic. It implies that you have thought out several critical aspects of your communication. These aspects can be recalled by the mnemonic device PRISTTOW:

- Purpose
- Response of the elderly
- Information needed ahead of time
- Steps and strategies
- Time
- Timing
- Outcomes
- What you want to say, what you can live with saying

PURPOSE

We have many wishes, hopes, and fears for our parents that may come out all garbled because they coexist in the same message.

> Louise, in her late forties, was the daughter of Maria, in her late sixties. Maria had been widowed for four years and had begun dating a man in the last few months. Louise, on the one hand, wanted her mother to have a full social life, but on the other would feel an occasional sense of betrayal of her departed father and also had some concerns that the man Maria was dating was more interested in her finances than anything else. Also, Louise was worried that if the two married and he fell into ill health, her mother would have to become his caretaker for many years.
>
> In part because she did not know what to say, Louise waited to discuss the situation with her mother until Maria announced that she would be getting married in two months. Louise, feeling pressured, wanted to tell her mother several things: (1) Louise felt Maria should not get married; (2) Louise did not trust the "new man" in Maria's life; (3) there were financial and legal considerations in second marriages that her mother should know about; (4) Louise had an article for her

mother to read about legal arrangements in second marriages; and (5) Louise wanted to be supportive of her mother. All of the concerns came out in a rapid-fire manner, leaving Maria feeling attacked by this barrage of concerns and information. It took several months for the two women to become comfortable in each other's presence.

Part of the trouble between Louise and Maria was that Louise had several important reasons for talking with her mother. It is common to have several purposes in talking with your parents. Even in pressure situations such as the one Louise faced, it is also helpful to sort them out *before* you have your discussion. In addition, you need to consider both your *role* and the *type of talk you are having*.

Your Role

The following are some of the most common roles in talking with your parents.

Giving Advice. Whether secretly or openly, we all think at times that we know what another person needs, wants, or would best benefit by. When we convey this to our parents, it is advice giving. Inasmuch as Louise would tell her mother that she should not get married, she was giving advice.

Advice has its place. Its place, however, is limited. Advice is one person's solution to another person's problems. If it is given as something that can be used or discarded without judgment or recrimination, it makes sense. When advice is a judgment, a way of blaming, or a "child-to-parent" communication, there are too many emotional strings attached for it to be useful.

Giving Opinions. Opinions differ from advice in that opinions represent your thoughts about an issue *without* implying that your parent should agree with you. Unlike pieces of advice, opinions do not necessarily promote a solution. Ideally, opinions are presented so that there is clarification of viewpoints and room for disagreement. In the case of Louise and Maria, when Louise told Maria her views or concerns about the new man in Maria's life without telling her mother what to do, she was giving opinions that could have been understood, even if her mother disagreed with them.

Giving Information. At times, you will be acting as a courier (or detective) for your parents, finding out information about services or entitlements and conveying what you learn to your parents. This role is extremely important in that you may have access to important information (or know how to get it) more easily than your parents. Information giving is relatively easy, provided you do not overstep your role to sneak in judgments, opinions, or advice, which will not be appreciated at the time your parents are expecting "facts and figures." Louise, for example, found out some information about prenuptial agreements and made it available to her mother, although when it was done along with advice and opinions, it probably was not well taken.

Listening. Listening is the fine art of attending carefully to the content, underlying feelings and thoughts of another person to promote better understanding. Understanding carries with it a sense of connectedness between the two people who are communicating, so watch out if you expect to be able to listen *without* some emotional connection between you and your parent. This is not to say that you should be overwhelmed by your parents' feelings if you listen but that, by attempting to understand your parent's meanings and feelings, you can feel emotional closeness and appreciate the wishes of your parents. For Louise, listening was very important, although it would have been better for her to listen first and then give her opinions, advice and information.

Decision Making. At times, children become decision makers for their parents, such as when they decide that their parents can no longer drive safely or need to have someone put in charge of their financial affairs. Louise did not end up in this position, although there are families in which legal action may be taken about remarriage. Being the decision maker is a difficult role and one that can carry guilt and remorse on all sides, in part because the older person is regarded as not being competent enough to make her or his own decisions.

Giving Your Blessing. This last role is interesting in that it can be viewed as the excuse for blame and judgment or, conversely, giving desperately needed approval to validate your parent, both of which are understandable, neither of which is a sign of a particularly healthy relationship. Rather, I think of giving your blessing as being appropriate when you, the child, are in a position to encourage your parent in making a major decision.

In the case mentioned earlier, Maria would have greatly appreciated Louise's blessing, but Louise was clearly not ready to give it until much later on. If Louise had gone along with her mother's need for approval, she would have been placating and both of them would have known it.

At the same time, Louise could have "blessed" Maria's being socially involved while maintaining a positive disagreement about Maria's choice of companion.

The Type of Conversation

Socializing. One important focus of talking with your parents is social, having the positive experience of each other's company. Some people think of this type of conversation as a "report card" visit, a cataloging of how and what we are doing, scrupulously avoiding anything that is important and avoiding any issues on which there can be serious disagreement, agreement, or sharing of feelings and perceptions. If you believe this to be true, think for a moment how you might want your own children (or grandchildren) to talk with you in the future. "Report card" visits are not much to look forward to, and are, for my money, more of a method of meeting social obligations than having meaningful social interaction.

Sharing. Sharing means that you are going to disclose some of your personal life issues, triumphs, or defeats to your parent in a way that opens you to being hurt and/or "stroked." Often, the children of older parents avoid sharing because of the fear of being hurt or misunderstood. This is understandable; but at the same time, without some real sharing between people, relationships are shallow and uncomfortable.

Deciding with Your Parents. This focus of talking with your parents is on aiding them in making *their* decisions as to how to take care of themselves, where to live, what to do, where to go, and so forth. Decision making can take time on both sides. Also, if your discussions focus on decision making, you may have to reassure your parents of your collaborative role, as different generations are not used to working *together*.

Warding Off Harm. When you ward off harm, it means that you anticipate a potential problem that your older relative is ignoring, either consciously or unconsciously. Of course, your discussion of future danger may be unwelcome, denied, or even incorrect. Also, for all intents and purposes, in this type of situation you are faced with a "confrontation," meaning that your view will not be the other's view but you are going to air it anyway; such was the focus of Louise and Maria's eventual talk about Maria's remarriage.

There are two goals in warding off harm. The first is getting your parents to believe or accept the possibility of danger of one type or another. The second is helping them to become active decision makers with you, so as to prevent, as much as possible, harm from befalling them. These goals are not easy to achieve and can be frustrating, but many of the skills and strategies in this chapter can help you succeed.

Straightening Out the Past. This topic can be considered a significant part of developing mature relationships with your parents. Straightening out the past should not be confused with the frequently disguised negative purpose of letting your parents have it for all the wrong they have done to you in the past. See Chapter 15 for further discussion of this topic.

Clarifying Your Role and Relationship. The nature of conditions faced by older persons and their families are such that, over time, the roles of children may need to change as the physical and emotional dependency of the elders increase. Help from outside of the family may be needed. Other family obligations may mean altering the types of assistance given. At times, the demands for care of older parents go beyond the resources, financial as well as human, of the children, who would be relegated to denying their own children and perhaps themselves in order to "give care."

Clarifying your role may mean setting limits, it may mean substituting paid services for care by family members, or it may mean functioning in a "new" role, including that of "case manager" or coordinating services for older parents. As you make these changes, it will help to talk about them with your parents. If you find yourself needing to alter your current role with your parents, you need to ensure that clarification is not perceived as a question of love. In addition, role clarification needs to be accomplished in a way that includes the needs of everyone, including your parent, you, and your family.

Armed with a better understanding of your purposes in talking with your parent, you should be able to cut down on miscommunication and misunderstanding about your motives. At the same time, knowing your purpose is not enough. You also need to know what to expect from your parent as well as information, some ideas on how to talk about the subject at hand, and what to do after you talk about it.

RESPONSE OF THE ELDERLY

It makes great sense to try to figure out how your parents may react to the topics you need to raise with them. This does *not* mean that you *know* what their reaction will be; instead, it suggests that you have considered how they may respond and are prepared for the "worst" as well as the "best." In the case of Louise, she was so caught up in her own concerns that she gave little thought to how her mother must have felt in taking a risk to become intimate with another man. It is also likely that Maria had mixed feelings about remarriage that reflected some of Louise's concerns and could have talked with Louise about them under the right circumstances.

INFORMATION NEEDED AHEAD OF TIME

Many of the discussions we want to have with our parents involve giving them information. It can be quite important to do some research on the topic of discussion beforehand, although you must take care that your parents do not feel railroaded or that you have gone "behind their backs." As one example, Louise did well to find an article on prenuptial agreements for Maria, although giving it to her mother at the same time they were discussing everything else may have made things worse.

STEPS AND STRATEGIES

How will the issue be raised? What aspects will you discuss? Do you need to listen to your parents' concerns before you say much? How will you convey your concern, care, and information or your point of view? Which skills, styles, and channels of communication will you use? These questions are critical in successfully approaching your parents about difficult topics. Louise, like many others, waited until circumstances dictated her talking with her mother, which in turn almost guaranteed unnecessary hard feelings and misunderstandings. When they had their discussion, there was little attempt on Louise's part to consider "strategic" and "skill" aspects, which was barely salvaged by finally listening to her mother's concerns and continuing to talk with her over the ensuing months.

TIME

Time refers to the amount of time, meetings, telephone conversations, and discussions you need to finish the business you raise with your older parent. It makes sense to take into account how frequently you are in contact, the nature of the issues, and the ease with which you can discuss similar matters, all of which can add to or detract from the amount of time you need for your discussions with your parents.

TIMING

Timing is related to but different from the time element. Timing, as the pundits put it, is everything. Specifically, it refers to choosing the point in a discussion (and in your daily life) at which you will raise the issues you want to raise.

One common problem of timing is faced by families who have to travel to see their older relatives and who tend to raise their concerns when the family gets together, usually on holidays. The problem is that these are frequently times when people's anxiety and emotions about the past are high. Another time when issues get raised is during a crisis, when no one can think clearly about what is going on, how things will be after they are settled, and what needs to be considered.

Even for families who live close to their older relatives, the timing of discussions is not always the best. Much discussion with older relatives does not take into account the need by the older relative to think over what has been said and have time to react to concerns, new information, or a "new" way a child is communicating.

OUTCOMES

Too often, we know an issue needs to be raised but are vague about what might happen next. Is it enough to put something on the table? Does action have to be taken today or not? If an issue is discussed, is it sufficient for one of you to "claim" that you will do something? Does a follow-up date (to be sure either of you did the things you said you were going to do) have to be set? Does a further discussion have to be scheduled?

WHAT YOU WANT TO SAY, WHAT YOU CAN LIVE WITH SAYING

This last aspect has two parts. The first is your coming to grips, *before* having the discussion, with what you really want to communicate with your older parent. If it is anger, anger about what? Is there an underlying feeling (guilt, hurt, disappointment, and so forth) that needs to be communicated? If it is advice, is it an opinion, or do you want at some level to "tell them what to do"? Some self-analysis and sorting out what you really want to say is best done *before* the discussion as a step in being congruent as well as to clarify your purpose and the outcomes you want.

Second, to say what you can live with saying means taking a look at the "bottom line," the things that you feel need to be communicated no matter what. The choice you make about what you can live with saying should be based on what you think is important for you, what is important for your parents, and what can be understood by your parents in their particular situation.

DEVELOPING STRATEGIES

Read the following story. Think how you might react in similar circumstances. Then look at how the PRISTTOW methods could help a daughter or son develop a communication strategy in a difficult situation.

> Ellen is a middle-aged woman whose two parents live nearby. Phyllis, her mother, can be very blaming and seems bitter from Ellen's perspective. Phyllis has maintained herself and her husband, Phillip, for years, but has arthritis and difficulty walking. While Phyllis has a reputation in the family for using guilt to manipulate others, Phillip has been her buffer, smoothing out anger and resentment from other family members. However, Phillip has now had a heart attack and is coming home to convalesce. He will need some professional nursing at home, as Phyllis is not physically capable of meeting his immediate needs. Ellen is worried that her mother's emotional style will drive the nursing aides out of the house and make her father's situation worse.

Ellen is faced with several decisions, starting with what she should say (and not say) to her mother. Does she talk to her mother about the aides, or does she wait and hope for the best? If she talks, how does she go about it?

Even if Ellen chooses to take some action, she is still faced with the possibility that Phyllis may drive the aides away because of her communication style. Using the PRISTTOW system of developing a strategy, the following would be useful for Ellen.

Purpose. In this case, Ellen's purpose is to "ward off harm"; that is, she wants to avoid a feared outcome. There is less of an immediate need to "make peace," give advice, or even be a sounding board. Ellen should focus her discussion on the major purpose and not get sidetracked into other issues.

Response of the Elderly. Ellen suspects that Phyllis is fairly unaware of her own emotional style and is not terribly introspective. If confronted about her style, Phyllis will deny it and become angry. Then, out of guilt, Ellen may feel compelled to provide more care than she really wants to.

Information Needed Ahead of Time. Because of the issues of trust and guilt, Ellen had better make sure she knows exactly what the aides will and won't do, as well as their hours and how to handle the possibility of their not showing up or a change in schedule.

Steps and Approaches. In a case like this, one recommended approach is for there to be a meeting between Ellen and Phyllis with the explicit agenda being how to handle the aides. Ellen should come prepared with specific requests and suggestions, such as, "If there is *any* trouble at all with an aide, discuss it with me first so we can decide what to do," or "I will call you after each aide's shift to find out how they did." Ellen may also need to have the physician state specifically to Phyllis that the aides need to be there but they must be allowed to do their job without her giving them too much "advice."

Time. This conversation should be held as soon as possible, allowing Phyllis to have a day or two to think over the content of the meeting and talk it over again with Ellen, who should be assertive about the limits being set.

Timing. This aspect is a bit harder to gauge, but it is likely that Phyllis will have considerable "venting" to do about the care her husband is being given, the failure of the rest of the family to be caring, and so forth. There may be value in letting her vent for a while, and then move the "meeting" over to the issues at hand.

Outcomes. Ellen needs an agreement from Phyllis to discuss problems with the aides with Ellen *before* confronting the aides herself. Ellen may need to check in with the aides as well to see if her mother is complying with the agreement.

What You Want to Say, What You Can Live with Saying. In this case, Ellen may have to say that there could be problems if the aides get "too much supervision" by the family, or may even have to tell Phyllis that she could make the aides mad. What Ellen has to say is that without aides, her father will be in worse shape than with them and that the family has to work with the home health agency to ensure good care.

SOME GUIDELINES FOR PROMOTING CHANGE

As you go about developing ways to talk with your parents, the following general guidelines for promoting change may be useful.

1. Pick your "fights" carefully; that is, choose issues that can be resolved or should be handled now.
2. Make it easy for your parents to say yes.
3. It's amazing how much you can accomplish if you do not take credit for everything.
4. Don't do others' work for them.
5. Don't promise more than you can deliver.

With these points in mind, there are a series of other guidelines that should be helpful to you in developing strategies for talking with your parents.

Including the Rest of the Family

> Eric, one of three children, was concerned about his mother, Bridgit. Bridgit was in her mid seventies and complained of pain while walking. Eric's sister, Brenda, was their mother's major caretaker and spent at least three days a week shopping, cleaning house, and visiting.
> Eric felt that Bridgit should see a geriatric physician and made a call to a geriatric clinic nearby for an appointment for his mother without consulting with Brenda. When Bridgit told Brenda about the upcoming appointment, Brenda's response was, "Why would you want to do something like that? They'll only find out things they can't do anything about."

Without realizing it, Brenda stopped her mother from going to the clinic. Eric would have done well to talk with his sister before taking action in his mother's "behalf."

Family members can aid or block talking with your parents, as Eric realized too late. As you consider talking with your parents, you need to consider not only your family norms and rules about communication, but also how the rest of your siblings, your aunts and uncles, and even your own children may react to the situation at hand. Are there people whom you need to bring into the discussions? When should you do this?

There are likely to be old rivalries or ambivalent feelings among siblings about your moving "closer" to your parent. Some may resent it, some may appreciate it. All will have some feelings about it, some of which are better aired and discussed than hidden, only to surface in ways that are unproductive.

You have the right to talk with your parents whether other family members want you to or not. However, your doing so will have implications and potential concerns for everyone. Expect there to be a variety of reactions, ranging from disbelief and denial to support and approval.

The following list of ideas, when used with the general guidelines for change outlined above, should help you in including your family:

- Find out who is supportive of your concerns and enlist them early to help you develop strategies. You may also want them present at your talks with your parents.
- Find out who is guilt-ridden and most defensive. Expect to spend some time with them to keep their personal issues out of the way of what you are trying to do.
- Consider having family meetings (preferably including your parents) to discuss what you are going to talk about with your parents.
- Identify rules, norms, and values in your family that support your talking with your parents, and use these as "reminders" when talking with the rest of the family.
- If there is serious unfinished business, address it directly before addressing the concerns about your parents.

Improving Trust and Understanding

Sharon's father, Maurice, had moved to Florida, where he lived in a retirement community. Sharon, age 35, had been concerned not only about his health, but also because he had become, in her words, "negative" where he had been positive in the past, including not liking to go out to restaurants, not being interested in hobbies, and being somewhat nasty to his friends.

After some thought about the issue, when on a visit, Sharon had a long talk with her father. She told him that she was concerned about both his physical and mental health and wanted him to get some help for himself. She went on calmly to say that she had noticed his "pessimism" and his lack of interest in activities, but also knew that he needed to make his own choice to get help or not. At the same time, she told him that unless he made a decision, she would continue to "bug" him about her concerns. "After all," she remarked with a smile, "what are children for?" They ended up laughing at her comment and, after further discussion during the rest of the visit, her father agreed to have a physical and "mental" checkup and made an appointment for the week after she left, which he kept.

Explain your purpose to your parents. Although you have presumably spent time preparing for discussions with your parents, they may not be at all prepared for you to talk with them about new things or in new ways. One step in helping them understand where you are "coming from" is to tell them why you are doing what you are doing. Sharon, by telling her father that she was wanted to talk to him about his condition, clearly stated her purpose.

Give a maximum sense of control to your parents. Control means that your parents have the right to think things through and make decisions, even if it means that the resulting decisions are not the ones you want. Control also means that your parents can maintain a sense of personal dignity and competence, even if the issue represents a loss of power, independence, and identity.

Ways of helping your parents maintain control are to include them in all decisions from the beginning, treat them as if they are capable of making decisions, and allow them talk about feelings and related concerns. Inasmuch as you are talking with your parents (as opposed to talking *to* them), you will also help them feel in control of their lives. Sharon followed this guideline quite nicely in talking with her father.

Learn how to be assertive when you need to be. Assertion is important when what you have to say needs to be presented even though your parent may not totally agree or like it. You should be prepared to be assertive about *specific* rather than general concerns, especially when you are dealing with setting limits or making your wishes known to a parental audience that is not totally receptive. For example, in the case mentioned earlier, Sharon was quite assertive about pursuing Maurice to get help.

Get specific next steps from each of you after a discussion on an important topic. Depending on your purpose, it will be important to get agreed-upon next steps, be it another discussion, a telephone call to make an appointment, or one of you getting some information about a particular service or program. If your purpose is to help your older parent make a major change in life-style or living situation, remember that there are many steps between deciding to move ahead on it and actually doing it.

Initially, getting some specific short-term outcomes will help the two of you see that "things are happening," as was the case for Maurice and Sharon once the doctor's appointment was set.

Give your parents information and materials that can help them talk better with you. This book is one possibility. There is nothing in it—or in others that focus on care of the elderly—that your parent should not know. In fact, much of it might help the two of you develop a common language to talk *about* your talking with each other. Older persons are just as eager as younger persons to get along well with their children. Getting information on how to do so is one good step in improving communication.

Use your talking as an opportunity to get to know your parents as they are now. Be open to the fact that the parent you are talking to today is not exactly the same person you talked to ten years ago, last year, or even last week. And just as you want them to know you as you are, you need to treat your discussions as an opportunity to get to know them as *they* are, not only for their physical and possible mental losses, but for their new strengths, changes in personality, and current sense of self-esteem.

Keep and use your sense of humor. One of the things that helped Sharon and Maurice work out their problems was Sharon's statement "That's what children are for," which was a nice turn on parental guilt. A sense of humor that is appreciative of both you and your parent and at the same time gives lightness, perspective, and balance to your discussions is a valuable part of your discussions. By contrast, negative, sarcastic, or depreciating comments will work against you and your parent and should be avoided.

STRATEGIES FOR COPING WITH FEELINGS

Jacky was the daughter of Irene, a woman in her eighties who had been diagnosed as having Alzheimer's disease. A family therapist whom Jacky consulted had asked her to bring her mother to one of their counseling sessions. The therapist focused the discussion on Jacky's relationship with Irene, paying particular attention to Jacky's feelings about her mother in the past and how hard it was to take care of her in the present. Irene sat through the entire session quietly, nodding her head but looking as if she really did not understand. However, as they were getting ready to leave, Irene turned to Jacky and said, "I am sorry for the pain I have caused you in the past." Without a direct discussion of feelings by Jacky, it is unlikely that Irene would have said those words.

Practice direct expression of feelings. Families often have strong rules about not telling others their positive or negative feelings. What happens then is that the messages about feelings become covert and frequently come out in defensive communication through blaming, placating, being superreasonable, or being irrelevant.

Direct expression of feelings is a substantial improvement over the "cold shoulder," abusive language, or, in the long run, avoiding contact with the other person. Even in the case of Jacky and Irene, there was potential for direct expression of feelings that could only be realized when there was an opportunity for both of them to talk.

Expect to feel pain and good feelings from time to time. Any human relationship has its share of both suffering and joy, distance and connectedness. Any meaningful set of discussions between two people who have shared contact over time may get to issues that were wonderful as well as those that were relative disasters. A direct and appreciative discussion can allow painful issues to become less painful and enhance the joy and bonds that also exist.

Your feelings may be honest reactions; they may be reactions to calibration or old wounds that have not healed. They may have to be dealt with, and you may find that some of the thoughts and beliefs underlying them are challenged. The first step in getting things straightened out will be to experience the feelings attached to the issue.

Listen to what your parents have to say. This has been mentioned previously in several guises. In order to communicate effectively with your parents, you need to understand what they are feeling and thinking as you talk to them. It is not enough to "know" ahead of time how they will react. You have to pay careful attention to see if your guesses are right or wrong. You also need to understand where they are "coming from" as one way of reminding yourself that the parts of their styles that are most difficult for you are *not* intended to make you feel bad or cause you harm, but are almost invariably statements about themselves, usually ones of lowered self-esteem.

Respect "museum hours." By "museum hours" I mean that you and your parent have years of history behind you with all kinds of artifacts, ancient bones, and rooms full of unfinished business. After some initial talks, you might want to push quite hard to clean up the entire museum before your parent is ready for it and find, instead, that the doors are shut, perhaps permanently.

Even museums are closed from time to time. Allow both of you to set the pace of what gets done in your talking together.

Appreciate the impact of potential changes on your parent. Many of the discussions with older parents focus on losses. Losses are of two types, "real" and "symbolic," even though they are frequently intertwined.

Real losses include things like money, a pleasant setting, and mobility. Symbolic losses include things like one's sense of identity, independence, mastery, decision making, self-esteem, status, and even the sense of being alive. The symbolic issues are ones that arise for many people faced with considering nursing home placement, hospitalization, or accepting a physical loss such as the loss of a limb, of hearing, or of vision.

One of the frequently used terms in the psychological and counseling literature on adapting to change is *acceptance*. Elisabeth Kübler-Ross, in her pioneering work on death and dying, has even labeled the idea of acceptance as a stage (and perhaps a "goal") in the death process. Handling the interaction of real and symbolic losses with a high sense of self-esteem can be considered another way of describing acceptance; that is, the older person adapts without losing self-concept, without remaining angry or depressed.

Acceptance of limitations in old age is not easy. We need to appreciate that what for us is a small change may be a large one for our parents because it represents a loss that cannot be replaced or may be a sign of their mortality. These things can be dealt with, but should not be brushed over as if they did not occur.

STRATEGIES FOR HANDLING DIFFICULT SITUATIONS

Paul, a man in his eighties, had become inappropriately suspicious of his wife, Martha. Every time she was in another room in their apartment with another man, even if it was their son, Martin, Paul started making comments like "What are you two doing in there?" Martha and Martin were hurt and surprised by Paul's behavior, but did not know what to say to him about it.

Finally, after some soul searching, Martin had a long talk with his father about how difficult it was for them to listen to these accusations. Martin pointed out that Paul might end up driving Martha away if this continued. It was at that point that Paul agreed, reluctantly, to see a geriatric specialist.

Martin and Martha were faced with a problem that required professional intervention. However, before they could pursue it, they had to begin to handle what was a very difficult situation. Without some discussion with Paul and Paul's agreement to seek help, the problem could have gone on for years without any relief.

Many situations with our older parents are difficult because there is often no easy solution or resolution of problems and feelings. Attempts to make changes do not always work successfully the first time or even the tenth time. Even if we succeed in mapping out a "perfect" strategy, unexpected complications may arise. The following strategies can help you begin to address difficult situations in talking with your parents.

Mentally, play "What if" and practice responses if necessary. This guideline is similar to "Expect the worst and be prepared to deal with it." You might be able to predict how your parents will respond to your wish to talk about your concerns for them. You should, with some luck, be able to come up with additional ways to handle responses they give that would ordinarily block you from getting what you want in the discussion. This guideline is meant to alert you again to the benefits of practicing new methods before taking them into the fray.

Reinforce the positive and ignore the negative. This phrase is taken from behavioral psychology, which has taught us, among other things, that others continue to respond in ways that are rewarded and give up responding in ways that are ignored. Paul's wife and son could have ignored his complaints and instead given him attention and encouragement when he was *not* being suspicious—although the nature of the situation was such that this alone would not have resolved things.

Too often, we forget the positive influence we can exert on others by smiling, touching, complimenting, telling them, "I really liked what you said" or "I really liked our discussion today—thanks." We should also remember that praise has to be meaningful and can include acknowledgment of the other's taking risks or even failed attempts to make contact with you.

Focus on the consequences of actions where arguing is futile. There are times in a parent-child relationship when arguments about who is right, what the facts are, and so forth are futile, leading only to bad feelings. In such cases, the guideline for discussion is to talk primarily about the consequences of the troublesome behavior or beliefs. In the case of Paul and Martin, Martin did well to continually remind his father that he would drive his mother out if he continued to hurl accusations at her.

Answer logical arguments with logic. At the same time, certain fears or concerns of older relatives are sensible, and, with the same respect you would want to give anyone else, you need to give them facts or information to decrease their reluctance to make needed changes. You will have to decide to what degree concerns are sensible and worthy of investigating for your parent.

Finding the information can be tedious and time-consuming. One of the issues here is to what degree you want to do it, to what degree your older parent can do it, and to what degree you can pay others (like information and referral services or social service agencies) to do some of the work.

If you are in an argumentative situation, look for common points of agreement. One of the dynamics of arguing is that at times a cycle of polar responses takes place, with each side becoming somewhat blaming and disagreeing with the other regardless of what is said. If you know you get into this type of situation with your parent, be sure to have some agreed-upon points that you can retreat to when you find you are getting polarized. Frequently, these will be specific aspects of the situation, not global (and unverifiable) feelings or perceptions.

Stick to specifics and avoid general statements. Statements such as "You need to change" or "You're not taking care of yourself" or "Your doctor is no good" or "You don't care about the rest of the family" are general statements. Although they can be put in "I" terms or said with care and compassion, they remain your conclusions about global and unverifiable circumstances. Your conclusions may be right or wrong, but if you put them in general terms, they may well be viewed as judgments about your parent and thus as advice or, at best, opinion.

You will do far better by focusing your discussions on specific issues, ones that can be verified or disagreed with without their becoming self-worth issues. Thus, "You need to change" can be discussed as "You need some information about banking accounts so you can get the most for your money." "You're not taking care of yourself" can be changed to "Mom, look, your room is dirty, and I know you have been wearing that dress for three days." And the statement "Your doctor is no good" can be changed to "Dad, let's look at the facts. You went to the doctor three times for the pain in your left leg, and he said it was due to your age. Is the right leg any older? Maybe you should get a second opinion."

Decrease calibration responses on your own part.

Laura lived near her parents, Joseph and Ellie. Joseph, in his eighties, was becoming more and more forgetful. Although Ellie could pretty much take care of him, Laura felt that Joseph would benefit from spending several hours a day at an adult day-care center, which would also help Ellie get some respite from the duties of constant care of her husband.

When Laura first raised the issue, Joseph and Ellie both were against it. Joseph claimed it would cost too much money, and Ellie claimed she could take care of him without any help.

Rather than go along with their refusal or blow up at them for being stubborn the way they "always" were, Laura spent some time considering how to make things work better. She spent time talking with her mother and directly addressing the question of her mother's ability to take care of her father, carefully explaining that the program was *not* "taking Ellie's place" and including Ellie as well as Joseph in planning which days he would go to the day-care center, how to pay for it, and other aspects of his participating in the program. She also spent time talking with her father and found out that he was afraid to go to the program, situated in a nursing home, because he thought his family was going to abandon him.

The transition to the adult day-care program was not easy. Laura's mother needed convincing that she was still in charge. Her father needed consistent assurance that he was not being abandoned. However, Laura was able to get her parents to make needed changes by avoiding a calibration cycle, listening to her parents' underlying concerns, and addressing these concerns using reassurance and assertive responses.

Calibration, as mentioned in Chapter 2, is the process by which subtle cues from one family member become the "triggers" for emotional responses and subsequent behavior by other family members. While it is possible to wish that your parent will change, or to try to work on changing together (including the possibility of seeking professional help), one part you can work on immediately is *your* response to calibration cycles. Several methods for doing so have been suggested at various places in this book. These include:

• Listening to your relative without judging
• Paraphrasing before reacting
• Being congruent in your communication
• Respecting the values of your parent
• Being specific

- Knowing the purpose of talking with your parent
- Finding underlying causes of your anger (e.g., other feelings)
- Using "I" language
- Being empathic as opposed to sympathetic
- Using an assertive style rather than being aggressive or passive

It is also possible to uncover specifically what triggers your calibration responses. Triggers can include words, tone of voice, eye contact, body movement, or any other aspect of communication style.

Once you have uncovered the specific triggers that set you off, you are in a position to decide how to change your response to them. One way is to talk about the *specific trigger* so as to find out what is actually going on in your parent's head when the trigger is given (another form of talking with your parent). Another way is talking to someone else about your response to your parents' triggers. You could talk to friends, a spouse, a confidant, or a mental health professional. You may also want to pursue behavioral and imagery training to learn how to relax instead of becoming upset when the calibration triggers occur. Finally, you and your parents could talk together with a family counselor or therapist about these patterns. The choices are yours.

RAISING THE TOPIC

As usual, you will do better to be congruent and straight about your discussion rather than hint around at the topic until your parents somehow or other figure out what you are getting at. At the same time, it makes sense to prepare them for the discussion by doing things like alerting them to the fact that you have something specific to discuss, such as saying, "Mom, I want to spend some time with you talking about my concerns for you. When is a good time to talk?"

This type of approach, by the way, is probably easier for your parent to hear then more *defensive* approaches, such as one of the following:

"Mom, you know you haven't been doing anything about moving, so we better deal with it now."

"By the way, Mom, I just happened to spend the last two weeks finding out everything about congregate living for the elderly and thought you would need this information, if you know what I mean."

"Why do you want to say *here?*"

"Mom, I know you are very independent and I shouldn't butt into your affairs, but maybe, maybe, please, pretty please, could you just let me give you a little information about some other housing options?"

Ideally, the topic should be raised when your parent makes some comment that naturally leads into a discussion, or when events suggest that the issues you want to discuss are on your parent's mind. Even at these times, I advise you to go a step at a time, asking questions about what your parents say rather than making them jump too far all at once.

One of the ways to approach sensitive topics is to arrange a time-bounded meeting in the near future to talk about the specific issue you need to discuss. Even as you do this, you should be supportive and reassuring that your intentions are to make things clear for all of you and that you are acting in good faith.

WHEN THINGS DO NOT GO WELL

One of the facts of life in talking with your parents is that things do not always go perfectly. Words get misunderstood, sensitive issues get triggered in ways neither of you is aware of, and emotional reactions get confused with issues of self-esteem. These will be the times when you wish you had never tried to do anything different and perhaps decide that the author of this book should be drawn and quartered!

Before giving up, I would recommend that you consider the question "What will I do if things don't work out well?" Use the following suggestions as guides.

- Check your purpose. Are you really talking about what you want to talk about? Are you saying what you want to say? If not, straighten it out for yourself before dealing with your parents.
- Are you hearing your parent? Or are you defensive? If you are defensive, try to decrease calibration or go for outside help.
- Is there some way to abandon the topic, acknowledging the difficulty and leaving the way open to discuss it at a later time when heads are cooler? (E.g., "This is hard for us to discuss now. It is important to me, so let's wait a while to bring it up again.)
- What about the discussion is difficult to you or to your parent? Are

these things that have to be addressed specifically before the overall issue is pursued again?

• Is a lack of trust getting in the way of "real" discussions? If so, can it be handled by the two of you alone, or are others, including professionals, needed to enable the discussions to continue?

• Are your family dynamics and/or values getting in the way? If so, how can these be addressed to make things go better?

• How are you coming across to your parent? (Maybe you are being perceived as incongruent, even if you feel you are congruent.) How can this be improved?

• Is this a time to talk to a therapist, counselor, family expert, clergy, physician, nurse, or someone who is sophisticated in these matters who can meet with family members and provide guidance?

The strategies in this chapter should give you some indications of how to go about talking with your parents when added to the skills discussed in Chapter 4. However, it is only the rare person who, after reading such a text, feels absolutely confident that he or she can overcome any obstacle and finally have a much needed discussion with a parent. Rather, many readers might think that what has been given so far is nice or interesting, but doesn't get to the hard issues, the ones fraught with obstacles and roadblocks at every turn.

That perception is exactly correct. Most human situations have roadblocks. The next chapter deals with some commonly encountered roadblocks in talking with your parents. Along with an analysis of the roadblocks, steps are given to help you to begin to overcome the ones that you face.

6

Roadblocks and How to Overcome Them

Arlene is the daughter of Francis, 78. Francis's husband died a year ago, and Arlene has been concerned about her mother living alone in a large house. At the same time, Arlene is afraid that Francis wants to come to live with her. Arlene is particularly fearful that her mother will dominate her life because "old people do that" and because Francis had also been domineering in the past.

Francis, on the other hand, does not particularly want to move in with Arlene. However, she thinks her daughter feels obligated to ask her and does not want to "hurt" her daughter's feelings by saying no if an offer is given. When they talk together, the subject of housing is never discussed.

Wilma, 82, had a stroke that left her with limited mobility. She has spent several months recovering, but still has to walk with a walker. She lives with her daughter, Edna. Wilma obviously feels embarrassed by her condition and will make statements such as "I'm a cripple" or "No one in the family thinks I'm any good." Edna, who wants to help her mother but is unsure what to say, says things like, "Oh, Mom, it's not so bad, you really have nothing to worry about," or (in an argu-mentative tone of voice) "Mom, they do too think you are fine."

Without realizing it, both Arlene and Edna are making things worse for themselves. Despite the best of intentions, each is putting a roadblock in the way of talking with her mother.

The roadblocks discussed below focus more on what *we* think, say, or do with our parents than what *they* do with us. I am not questioning that our parents may be difficult to handle because of their personal style or personalities. However, even in the most difficult circumstances, our job is to make sure we do not make things harder than they already are.

FIVE TYPES OF ROADBLOCKS

There are five types of roadblocks that can work against talking with your parents:

- Preconceived notions
- Behavior that promotes ineffective communication
- Guilt-related roadblocks
- Behavior that sabotages change
- Other family members

Preconceived Notions

Thinking of Your Parents As Elderly. In Chapter 2, I discussed some of the stereotypes that people have about the elderly. Five related beliefs that can ruin any chance you have of relating to your parents are these:

1. She/he is rigid *because* she/he is old.
2. She/he won't listen to what I say *because* she/he is old.
3. Her/his mind is gone *because* she/he is old.
4. She/he wants to run my life *because* she/he is old.
5. She/he is irrational *because* she/he is old.

There is little question that some older persons (like some younger persons) have these characteristics. Some older persons are rigid and have a great deal of difficulty listening to what their children try to tell them. Some have mild and some have severe cognitive losses. Some older persons feel a need to try to control the actions of others, and some are not sensible at times.

However, once the problem is thought of as being due to *aging*, then there is a sense that things cannot change and a loss of hope that any real communication or relationship can be developed. The odds are fairly great that the rigid or nonlistening older person has been like that for some time. (If, in fact, there has been a dramatic change in personality, that in itself is good reason to get the older person evaluated by a competent and geriatric-sensitive physician or nurse clinician.)

At the risk of making a sweeping statement, I propose that *no personality style, type, pattern, or particular habit, defensive manner, or anything else that we could call part of personality in older people is "because they are old."* The more you believe that an old person is rigid or helpless and cannot change because of age, the less you will be willing to try to relate to your older parent.

In the beginning of this chapter, one of Arlene's roadblocks is her belief that her mother will dominate her because "old people are that way." With this belief, Arlene gives herself little reason to check her perceptions out with her mother. After all, why bother to discuss something that cannot change and will only be denied?

Overcoming the roadblock of preconceived notions requires you to think differently. For example, if Arlene reframed difficulties with her mother from being due to her age to her "being the way she is," she could begin realistically to handle her mother's responses.

Expecting Failure. Nothing breeds failure like expecting to fail. Going into an encounter with your parents expecting that nothing positive can happen is highly likely to make you put up your own defenses, which in turn may cause your parents to put theirs up, and you will be off to the races before you know it, having actually helped a feared outcome come to pass.

If you find yourself with an expectation of failure in your discussions with your parents, try to prevent it from becoming a self-defeating attitude. It may help you to answer the following questions:

• Specifically, what am I expecting to happen?
• Specifically, how will I know if "it" happens?
• Specifically, how will I know if "it" did *not* happen?
• Specifically, what do I *want* to happen and how will I know if what I want is happening?
• Specifically, what can I do to
  —feel less hopeless if "it" happens?
  —ensure small successes in "hopeless" situations?
  —make sure I do not contribute to the "bad" outcome?

Setting Expectations Too High. This roadblock is the flip side of expecting to fail. Setting expectations too high means that, no matter what happens, the result will seem negative because it doesn't match what you *hoped* for.

High hopes are one thing, but high *expectations* can lead to big letdowns even though positive changes are taking place. If you find yourself having high expectations, you would do better to realize that your expectations actually are your wishes. They should not be confused with the realities, whatever changes are taking place.

Behavior That Promotes Ineffective Communication

This second group of communication roadblocks is particularly effective in promoting *poor* communication and results in poor relationships between you and your parents. Most of these behaviors are done outside of your awareness, but their effect is deadly nonetheless.

Patronizing. Patronizing is the fine art of talking to another person as if he or she were less than functional. The most obvious ways of patronizing an older person are by baby talk, an overly "sweet" tone of voice, a slightly singsong manner, and a "knowing" smile that says, "You poor dear, I understand that you are not really competent, but we'll pretend, won't we?" Other forms of patronizing can be done verbally, like using *we* instead of *you* (my favorite is "It's time for 'our' bath") or explaining things that do not need explaining.

Patronizing has several forms. The message to the recipient, however, is remarkably similar: "You are less than human. You don't count."

Unfortunately, while others are painfully aware of patronizing, the people who do it are rarely aware of how they are coming across. You may need exquisitely friendly feedback from a spouse, a friend, your children, or even your parents themselves to find out if you are being patronizing with them.

Patronizing may be the result of your trying to simplify information and feeling uncomfortable about doing it, being afraid of what your parents may say to you, a difficulty expressing some concerns about your parents, or your thinking that this is the way to talk to an old person. These beliefs and concerns can then be addressed directly and will need some consideration if you are to stop putting up this roadblock in talking with your parents.

False Reassurance. When our parents are faced with difficult and trying circumstances, one of the great temptations is to "make them feel better" by making one of a series of statements that are, in part, untrue. Inasmuch as the message is partly untrue, it can be labeled "false reassurance." Some examples include:

"Don't worry, everything will be all right."
"You have nothing to be depressed about."
"You're not really afraid."
"You'll get over it."

As you may recall from the beginning of this chapter, Edna, in trying to help her mother, gave her false reassurance ("You really have nothing to worry about.") Although Edna meant well, the impact of that statement in all likelihood was to make her mother believe that something was really wrong with her.

In fact, when people are worried about something, their worry is legitimate in that they feel anxious, scared, or depressed. This does not mean that no reassurance can be given. We can give reassurance that

- We care.
- We will be there.
- There is hope (which can take many forms even in the worst of circumstances).
- We will listen.

If you find yourself giving false reassurance, practice making genuinely reassuring statements of these kinds, which are not false reassurance. Then try them with your parents, and pay attention to their impact. My guess is that, quite often, they will give you better results than using false reassurance.

Withholding Information. In many families, information is withheld from certain members for a variety of reasons. Children may not be told about the circumstances of deaths; older relatives may not be told the sad truths about family members because it would somehow hurt them. Wanting to keep information from people is understandable, but the practice is overused in families.

> Emma, in her mid-eighties, had a chronic heart problem that led to her being placed in a nursing home. Her husband, Jim, used to visit daily until he became sick. He finally died, but no one in the family wanted to tell Emma for fear that she "could not take it."
>
> Emma became quite depressed because her husband wasn't visiting. He was, to her knowledge, sick in the hospital, and the rest of the family acted "strange" whenever she asked them questions about her husband.
>
> Finally, one of her sons told her the truth. She was actually relieved to know her husband was not suffering all those weeks, but felt quite upset and angry that she had not been told in the first place. "What do you think," she asked her children, "that I'm too far gone to care?"

This case shows quite clearly the difficulties in withholding information from an older parent. Despite the family's good intentions, Emma knew something was going on, thought things to be even worse, in a sense, than they were, and also took the withholding of information to be a statement about her.

The issue of withholding information is somewhat thorny. It would be ridiculous to insist that every older person be told everything about their conditions, circumstances, and so forth. However, the withholding of information invariably brings with it a judgment that the older person is not capable of hearing information that he or she has a moral (and perhaps legal) right to hear. In addition, if and when your parents discover that information has been withheld, their reaction is, understandably, likely to be one of distrust and anger.

When faced with the question of withholding information from your parent, ask yourself the following question: "Would I want the information withheld from me by my family without my consent?" A second guide is to decide what your relative is entitled to know regardless of how you might think it will affect him or her. Finally, if you decide that difficult information should be shared, spend time deciding how to share the information in an accurate and supportive manner.

Deciding for *Your Parent.* A related roadblock occurs when the family makes decisions *for* the older adult. Decisions that get made for older adults are implicitly thought of as being outside their capability or as decisions that they cannot make wisely themselves. How many families have seriously considered nursing home placement *without* consulting with the person who will be placed in the facility? How many families have decided that hospice care is called for *without* informing the person who is dying? How many families have decided that Mother will live with one or more family members, and *then* discussed it with Mother?

Each of these cases is understandable. Each also suggests that the family is avoiding confrontation or dealing with feelings. Unfortunately, the negative results of such decisions are too often felt afterward by family members, professional service providers, and others who are around the older person. I cannot think of many instances when deciding for an older person improved communication and relationships.

The obvious way to overcome this roadblock is to make decisions *with* the older person. To do otherwise is potentially a violation of your parent's rights.

Using Power Plays. Power plays are any attempts to influence decisions by implicit threats of giving, taking away, or otherwise controlling resources, including affection, money, time, and services such as chores. Examples of power plays are these statements:

"Mom, if you live with us, we'll charge you no rent."
"Dad, I will only shop for you if you move."
"Mom, we will only take you with us on vacation if you go to the doctor first."

Power plays can get the results you want and may have to be used if a life-threatening situation has arisen. But for the most part, the price paid is that trust is decreased and your parents feel unduly pressured to do or say something they do not want to do or say. If you expect to relate to your parents on an adult basis, you cannot use control over resources or affection as the way to get them to listen to you or do your bidding.

Arguing. Arguing is the fine art of turning two people into adversaries rather than simply people who disagree. The process can rapidly become one in which blame-related statements emerge that have nothing to do with the matter at hand but are more a reflection of previous conflicts. For example:

"You don't know what's best for you."
"Why don't you listen to me?"
"I'm right and you're very, very wrong."
"You're just obstinate, that's your problem."

Arguing also implies a question of power. That is, it becomes more important to be "right" than to get the problem solved. If, by chance, you are "correct," then for your parents to "give in" means a loss of self-esteem which will not make them particularly eager to agree with you.

At the same time, arguing is not the same as disagreement. It is quite sensible for people to disagree. The question, when there is disagreement, is how to handle it, how to make your points or ideas known, and how to listen to the other point of view without feeling that your self-esteem is at stake.

So what do you do if you find yourself arguing on a regular basis with your mother or father? Arguing can also be viewed as as an "escalation" of a calibration cycle. That is, you (or your parent) say something that somehow triggers off a stronger emotional response from the other person, which comes out in his or her next statement, which in turn triggers a stronger emotional response from you, and so forth until there is a good deal of anger and irrational behavior.

What you need to do is to break your part of the cycle, to learn to deescalate. Ways to do this include the following:

- Practice a "relaxed" response. (You can do this by visualizing "relaxed" images, physically relaxing your "tight places," or practicing deep breathing. You can even practice by telling yourself to relax while imagining argumentative statements made by your parent.)
- Ask for clarification.
- Paraphrase.
- Ask your parents (a) what *they* want or (b) some of their reasons for feeling as they do. (Be sure when you do this that you don't push your own views in by saying such things as "Why don't you feel —— about it?" or "There's really no reason to feel ——, so why do you feel that way?")
- Make meta-comments: "I cannot tell you what I think, because if I disagree with your position, I think you would treat it as a personal attack."
- Talk about your feelings: "I feel angry right now."

Not all of these approaches are guaranteed to make things better, but each carries with it the possibility of allowing the argument to evolve into a more productive discussion. I encourage you to discuss these with other people and to practice them in a role-playing situation with another person, having your partner act out the part of either you or your parent. This will help you figure out which approaches fit your circumstances, temperament, and abilities.

Arguing the Unacceptable. Along with arguing, another roadblock to communication is pushing for an unacceptable alternative when your parent is dead set against it. Examples include nursing home placement, a change of residence, a severe change in life-style (like giving up smoking or changing eating habits because of diabetes), or even hiring someone to do housework or prepare meals.

If it happens that the "unacceptable" is the only option, you are faced with two questions. First is how to prepare your older relative for the "inevitable." Second is how to present the alternative.

Preparation may only need to be a few minutes of conversation focusing on the realities of your parent's situation, including the dangers of continuing the status quo. The response to this may well be denial, anger, and hostility. However, avoiding the discussion because of these expected reactions may not only delay the pain but it may also intensify it later on for everyone concerned.

If the situation is not an immediate crisis, you might focus on preparing your parents for the difficult decisions they have to make. Here is where focusing on the consequences of behavior assertively but caringly can help promote change over time. You may need to continually remind your parents that you are not attacking their self-worth but rather are concerned about their health and safety because you are their son or daughter, because you do care, and because you would feel bad if something bad happened to them. If there is no crisis, your parents will have time to think over what you said after the discussion, which in turn may lead to change even though it may not be acknowledged as coming from you.

Guilt-Related Roadblocks

> Fred, an engineer in his mid-forties, had been laid off during a recession in the aerospace industry. A few weeks later, he went home for a visit with his parents. His father, as was customary in his family, asked him how things were going. Fred didn't know what to say. He felt like a failure, he felt guilty about the layoff, and he thought that his parents would not approve of his not having a job to support his family. Instead of answering his father, he quickly changed the subject. After the visit, he had only minimal contact with his parents until he got a new position three months later. His parents, in the meantime, were worried that he was getting divorced or was sick, or "worse."

Guilt has been mentioned several times in the course of this book. It seems that feelings of guilt are among the most common reactions of family members in dealing with their elderly relatives.

Guilt is not a single, simple emotion. It is the physical and verbal reaction to a personal sense of having violated a rule combined with a need to punish oneself for violating the rule. For example, Fred changed the subject when his parents asked him about his work and avoided contact with them until he found a new job as one way of attempting to handle his guilt over being a "failure."

This book is not about how to relieve yourself of all your guilt so that you can become a happy and responsible adult. It is important, however, to look at the problems that come about when your discussions with your parents are based on guilt—that is, out of your own feelings about avoiding mistakes and self-punishment—instead of on figuring out what is best for both of you.

Guilt is painful. Its manifestations can be somatic (including feelings of dread or anxiety, sweating, and sleep problems), behavioral (overeating, drinking too much, going on binges), or verbal (talking over and over to oneself or others about a problem). As we go through life trying to compensate or relieve our guilt about our parents, we may do things like spend too much or too little time with them, or put the wrong resources into the older person's situation (as when a family insists that the parent live with them even though the parent does not want or need to). The list of guilt-related feelings and actions by families of the elderly is quite large. Some of these roadblocks are avoidance, being judgmental, moralizing, manipulating others, using guilt, and seeking parental approval.

Avoidance. One of the more common guilt-related roadblocks to talking with parents is avoidance. It can mean changing a topic of discussion or actually avoiding your parents' company. Avoidance is not the same as setting limits, because truthful explanations are not given as to why you are avoiding a topic, a visit, or contact with your parents. At the same time, avoidance is an attempt to decrease discomfort that will work to a limited degree, although many people who avoid their parents still feel guilty for choosing this particular strategy.

One result of avoiding contact with your parents is that they invariably feel that you are deliberately hurting them. Avoidance may be all you feel you can do in certain circumstances, and you certainly have an inherent right to avoid contact with people as you wish, but avoidance will effectively block communication and improved relationships.

Being Judgmental. Being judgmental means that you are, by word, voice tone, or even body and face position, making an absolute judgment on a person, thought, or deed. Frequently, we are judgmental when the concern is emotionally charged for us and we feel the need to control the situation at some level by "deciding" what is right and what is wrong.

That overly harsh sense of right and wrong is the guilt-related aspect of this roadblock.

Think of what a discussion might be for an elderly woman and her daughter discussing the possibilities of a new apartment for the mother:

Mother: You know, dear, I was thinking about moving. I actually went over and looked at the apartments over on Regency Drive.

Daughter: [Drawing her eyebrows together, pursing her lips] That's not much of a choice.

Mother: I suppose a condominium would be nice, too.

Daughter: I think it's ridiculous how those owners charge too much for monthly maintenance fees.

Mother: I wonder what the senior housing units are like in town.

Daughter: [Scowling, lips pursed] It's your choice, of course.

In this case, the daughter, who is trying to help, is coming across as quite judgmental and is likely to make her mother feel foolish for even considering a move. The sad part is that the daughter may, in the long run, "decide" that her mother really did not want to move without realizing her own influence on the situation.

If you find yourself being judgmental, you may have to do some thinking away from the situation. What are you really concerned about? What are the fears or concerns that underlie your need to pass judgment about what is happening? Is it a question of control? Are you having difficulty with an option? Is there some irrational rule operating, such as "I must always make the best decision for my parent, who tried to make the best decisions for me?" (The last rule is a bit irrational in that it implies that you always have to be right as well as that you should decide *for* your older relative.) With a little diligent searching, you may find the underlying rule or rules that trigger your being judgmental and go about deciding, as an adult, whether or not these rules fit for you or if you need to change them.

Moralizing. Moralizing is similar to being judgmental, only it focuses more on the appropriateness (and "morality") of the other's behavior. How many smokers are there who have heard endless sermons about how they are killing themselves, and who for the most part disregard them? Moralizing also implies that the preacher (and believe me, the person hearing it feels that the other is preaching) is somehow at a higher moral level than the person being preached to.

With a moralizing approach, you might get some short-term changes in your parent. You might be able to shame them into doing things differently. At the same time, you will have accomplished nothing of any use in establishing open communication and a trusting relationship.

Many of us have difficulty with parents who are still moralizing at *us* thirty years after they had their shot at raising us to be responsible and decent human beings. Old, residual reactions of guilt can emerge after only a few minutes of discussion about almost anything. Becoming neutral about your parents' moralizing is the goal in cases where their style "gets" to you. Ways to decrease the impact of their moralizing include all of the skills in decreasing calibration responses, such as talking to your parents about their style; talking to peers, clergy, physicians, nurses, or counselors; getting professional help from a therapist; or joining a self-help group.

Manipulating Others. "Others" here refers to your parents, your other relatives, and, potentially, the professionals who may be involved with your parents. There is a mighty temptation to use against them the types of manipulations you discover they are using to "control" you, in a kind of "fight fire with fire" response. The forms this can take can be quite complicated, including using intermediaries to take messages to your parents, withholding affection unless your wishes are met, or using the professionals to push for what you want without directly dealing with your parents.

This type of manipulation too often brings with it resentment, guilt, and other hard feelings. It is quite understandable for us to want to return "an eye for an eye," but the result, in terms of the relationship, will be hurt and low trust.

Using Guilt. There is a related temptation to use guilt to move a guilt-producing older person to change something in her or his life. Frankly, it must be admitted that guilt *can* be used to make others to do certain things.

In deliberately using guilt to get another person to change, we are in effect stating that the change is *so* important that we are willing to put our love and affection on the line to produce it. There are situations in which this may seem warranted, but they are far fewer than the temptation to use guilt would lead us to believe. I would rather have us, after carefully considering the potential risks and harms, give our parents full rights and responsibilities (and information and love and concern) to make decisions, to be their own persons, and to get to know us as we are now. Using guilt-related approaches does not allow these options.

Seeking Parental Approval. This last guilt-related roadblock is one that exists for many adults. Even though they are mature and may have children of their own, there can still be a tremendous need for parental approval of their achievements or of how they live their lives, with guilt being a considerable part of their emotional reaction if parental approval is not forthcoming.

It is one thing to appreciate praise from others or have an adult sense of achievement mirrored in how your parents view you and your life. It can be quite damaging in the many difficult situations facing older persons for the children to lose their own sense of responsibility and distance and to make their parents' approval of their actions their primary motivation, rather than trying to keep the well-being of the parents and themselves in harmony.

Overcoming Guilt-Related Roadblocks. Overcoming guilt-related roadblocks is not a simple matter, in part because guilt is well learned and can be triggered by many things that your parents say or do as well as your own thoughts and reactions to what they are saying. The following suggestions represent some initial steps in handling these. If you find they do not work for you, consider talking about your "guilt traps" with others, including your spouse, family, clergy, or professional counselors or therapists. Guilt can be transformed into positive responsibility.

With this in mind, you can do the following:

- Identify your own guilt-related rules and rewrite them to be more "adult." (Hint: Many of the guilt rules have lots of "shoulds" or "nevers" that need to be transformed into "like tos" or "whenever possibles.")
- Use "I" language (this is particularly effective in decreasing moralizing).
- Talk with your parents about how you are feeling (make meta-comments).
- Argue with yourself: "Does my punishment really fit the 'crime'?"
- Examine what you think you might fear that leads you to use guilt-related communication rather than being congruent with your parents. Use this as a beginning of some work on transforming your fears into learning about yourself, your family's past, and what you want to be as an adult.

Behavior That Sabotages Change

Another set of roadblocks includes those which make sure that if things start to get better or get good, they will not stay that way for long.

Overlooking Small Changes. Too often, change starts to manifest in small ways, like a statement that is not made, blame that is not given, or praise and encouragement that come about for just a little while. Like flowers growing from seedlings, changes need to be nurtured and respected even if they are small. You certainly know how hard it is for you to try new ways of talking with your parents. Please, for the sake of improved relationships, be equally sensitive to their attempts to make contact and move in new directions in their discussions with you.

Making an Inch a Mile. At the same time, small changes do not mean that everything you always wanted from your parents (and never wanted to ask) is waiting around the bend and will be gushing forth in a spirit of unconditional giving. A few faltering steps toward looking for new housing, a decision to have one meal a day delivered, an agreement to go to a physician—all of these are important beginning steps, but they are just that, beginnings. The older person may renege after initial steps, just as you or I might. Your parents may need an entirely different set of supports and information to continue with something once they have made the initial steps to find out about it. Discussions about your family history may get rocky at times, even if the initial talk goes well. An inch is an inch, no more or less.

Other Family Members

Diane, the mother of two young children, had taken her own mother, Emily, in to live with her. Emily had arthritis and diabetes, but otherwise was in good health and led an active life in the community. Sylvia, Diane's older sister, lived in another state, called weekly and came for occasional visits. Whenever she visited, Sylvia would complain to Diane about Diane's house and the way she cared for their mother, saying that Diane did not do enough for Emily.

Diane was surprised by Sylvia's behavior, but suffered quietly for several visits, in part because she felt guilty about not meeting all of her mother's needs. Finally, when she could take it no more, she had a heart-to-heart discussion with Sylvia, telling her directly that she thought Sylvia was feeling guilty about not being near their mother and leaving much of the care to Diane. Sylvia, after some thought, agreed with Diane. Together, they decided that Sylvia should be brought into any decisions that Diane and Emily might make about living arrangements in the future.

It is not uncommon in families with an elderly and frail older person for one person to take on the primary caregiving role. Others, however, may feel, out of obligation, duty, or even guilt, that they should get highly involved when they are on the scene. They may, at some level, resent the primary caregiver's getting "close" to the parent. They may feel guilty about their absence (the primary caregiver is frequently living close by) but transform it into anger about how the caregiver is doing his or her tasks, or even underestimating (or overestimating) the older person's abilities.

If you are in the position of being the primary caregiver for your parents, you may want to help other family members stay included in major decisions, as well as play meaningful roles in whatever needs you are going to meet for your older relative. You can, however, expect that past conflicts may well flare up again, especially if a crisis occurs. It is not uncommon for old sibling rivalries to emerge as to who was the best child, the favored child, and so forth. You cannot expect that everyone will lay down previous grievances just because Mother or Father is sick, needs to talk about something, or even is going into a nursing home. The family history, rules, and norms still prevail, at times even more strongly than ever.

It will also be useful to remember (if you can) during the times of intense emotionality that your brothers, sisters, aunts, uncles, and own children may be angry, may be guilt-inducing, may even be working against the best interest of your parent; but it is rare indeed that they are doing so for "negative" reasons. Effective communication can help you sort out the underlying feelings and norms that hinder you from working on the family problems you face. This in turn means that you have to be as good a listener with other family members as you would be with your parents.

Taking Sides. One of the most common dynamics in families is that of taking sides. By taking sides, you have, at some level, chosen to be "loyal" to one or more persons in the family, and you believe that somehow they are "right," "correct," or the victims of others in the family.

Taking sides may mean choosing in favor of either your parents or other family members who may want to decide for them or withhold information. It can be extremely difficult to refrain from taking sides in this type of family situation. There can be tremendous pressure to go along with your spouse, sister, or brother, especially when you know there will be old wounds opened when you do not go along. You may hear remarks like "You always were the one to disagree" or "See, you never could take suggestions from me" or "You always tried to act like the big brother."

These salvos will hurt. You will be tempted to escalate them by responding with your own. My suggestion, and it is not an easy one to follow, is to be prepared for the salvos and have deescalating responses for each of them, primarily through the use of assertion and/or reflection. For example:

"I may have disagreed with you in the past. I have been wrong, too. However, I really believe this is right this time."

"You must feel that I am not listening to what you have to say because I do not agree with all of it."

"It's hard for both of us to separate old feelings about each other from the points involved here."

Another potentially effective strategy is to be sure you have an ally with you when talking with your family members. An ally could be your spouse, a friend, a professional, or another family member, whose job it is to make sure you are not escalating and who can act to meta-comment or even be assertive with other family members who get you too upset to take care of the business at hand. Getting an ally to work with you may take time and preparation, but the strength of two voices and two minds can be quite powerful and useful to a family in crisis or at emotionally difficult times.

Guilt, Family History, and the Present. One of the things that comes up when families focus on the concerns of their older relatives is promises, pledges, concerns, omissions, and commissions that have taken place in the past around the relative in question. When a crisis takes place, you might hear others saying things like:

"You promised you would always take care of Mother, that she would never be in a nursing home, that she would never have to go to a hospital."

"You never did much for Father, and it seems you are doing the same now."

"You always got the most from them, so you should give the most back."

These are all examples of how guilt and prior history can add tension to the present. As a rule of thumb, the more you can get your family system to separate itself from unresolved questions of the past, the better off you will be in getting them to focus on the questions of the present. In order for others to see the current concerns in their real light, they have to get beyond who loves whom and who owes what to whom.

The essential precondition for having "straight" conversations with family members is mutual trust. When trust is low, decisions will be made by whoever has the power or authority to make them. It might make sense, in some cases, to try to straighten out old grievances *before* dealing with matters concerning elderly relatives.

The question of how to handle other family members is complicated, and well worth considering in that family members may be roadblocks or potential allies in your attempts to talk with your parents. As with the other types of roadblocks, we can transform them into something less forbidding and spend the time necessary to create trust and a sense of appreciation and understanding before trying to make the family work on specific issues with older relatives.

The list of roadblocks in this chapter is long but is not complete. There are easily as many ways to work against communication as there are to work for it. I hope that you have spotted some of the ones you might be "guilty" of committing and have gotten some ideas as to how you might want to work on them before venturing forth to talk with your parents.

7

Talking about Housing

Susan is the 60-year-old daughter of Anne-Marie, who is in her early eighties. Susan has been increasingly worried about Anne-Marie, who has failing eyesight and arthritis. Cans and sometimes doors are hard for her to open, and she has difficulty reaching objects on high shelves. Susan thinks something should be done about her mother's living arrangements but does not know what to say to her mother, who is embarrassed by her physical losses.

Many persons find themselves in circumstances similar to Susan's. They are concerned about changes in their parents' situations that may mean a change in housing arrangements, but do not know how to talk to their parents about their concern or lack appropriate information to help plan needed changes, including altering an existing residence to accommodate their parents' limitations. They are also caught between the need to talk to their parents about housing-related concerns and personal issues that make the discussions difficult to initiate.

Housing is one of the most complex issues facing the elderly. Housing choices are influenced by economic factors, health factors, availability of types of housing arrangements, knowledge about housing options, and "eligibility" factors, which can range from having an income low enough to qualify for subsidized housing to having an income high enough to pay for living in a retirement community. All of these aspects combine to make discussions about housing necessary and, at the same time, potentially fraught with emotional, legal, and economic difficulties.

FACTS AND FIGURES

As surprising as it may seem to younger people, about 95 percent of all older people live in the community (as opposed to institutions). Most older people (72 percent) actually own their own homes, and almost all of these people (84 percent) have no mortgage and own their homes "free and clear."

There are certainly older persons who do want to move in with their children and do so. However, studies of older persons' preference in housing show that that most older persons do not want to live with their children but would rather live independently. In the aggregate, older persons have as strong a wish for independence as their children do.

Types of Housing

There is considerable confusion about "types" of housing for older persons. In part this is because there is no agreed-upon language or system for describing all the options. Also, the specific options available in an area vary considerably, some being present, some being so overused as to be unavailable for practical purposes, and some actually being unable to be utilized because of ignorance, zoning restrictions, or municipalities' rules.

The following listing of *types* of housing options is thus a guideline for considering what might be best for an older relative.

Owned Housing. The most common form of housing for the elderly is *home ownership.* It is commonly defined as legal possession of and residence in the same single-unit (or, occasionally, double- or triple-unit) dwelling. Homeowners are responsible for upkeep, utilities, and taxes, even if the mortgage is paid off. Homes represent one of the major assets of older persons, but as assets they are not easy to have access to without creating a new mortgage or selling the house.

Several interesting options are beginning to be developed that allow homeowners to maintain possession of and residence in their homes and give older homeowners access to some of the money (equity) in their homes. One is a *reverse mortgage,* a process by which a bank or other financial institution gives older persons money each month until their death, the sum of which is paid back to the bank or institution at the end of a specified period of time or from the eventual sale of the person's house.

A second idea is a *sale-leaseback* model, in which the older person sells the house to another party (usually below the going cost of the house) and then has a formal lease on the house until his or her death. The new owner takes on all financial responsibilities such as taxes and maintenance, and the homeowner negotiates a monthly "rent" for living in his or her own house.

Another idea is *house sharing,* in which an older person with a home takes on a housemate, who pays rent for the right to share the home or gives services (e.g., shopping, housekeeping, companionship) in return for living in the owner's residence. In this case, the homeowner is basically renting space to a roommate. Frequently, people wishing to share a house utilize local clearinghouses (often nonprofit agencies) that help match people with appropriate needs and resources.

A final housing option available to homeowners is to modify the structure of their homes to accommodate their physical needs. Redesigning sleeping quarters, putting a bathroom on the first floor, and changing doors, appliances, and cabinets are all possibilities that can make a home into a functional unit for an older person. Many of the features put into apartments for handicapped persons can be adapted for individual houses, as well as apartments or condominiums.

Condominiums are units of housing (usually attached) that are owned by individuals but have certain common costs (such as maintenance, grounds, and certain recreational and utility costs) borne by the owners of all the units. Condominiums have increased in popularity since the early 1970s, with apartment buildings being converted into owned units. Condominiums have become one option for older persons who are able to both carry a mortgage and pay a monthly common charge in return for not having to make major repairs or keep up the grounds of their dwelling.

Rented Housing. Rental arrangements can include an independent apartment, an apartment attached to the home of a family member (often called an "in-law" apartment), or the rental of a townhouse, another person's condominium, or a house. In all cases, the older person is living independently but does not own the space in which he or she lives.

Moving into a family dwelling is obviously different from moving into an apartment in a large complex. Not only is there much more contact and potential disruption of family routine, but in order to have such an apartment added to an existing dwelling, there has to be careful checking of zoning and housing codes to see if such an alteration in one's home is legal.

With rented space, altering living arrangements to accommodate the physical condition of an elderly person needs to be negotiated with the owner of the property. There will be questions of who should pay for changes such as rails for toilets, new lighting, or the installation of special doors, telephones, and other aspects of the physical environment. Families should find out building code requirements and any tax or other advantages for landlords who help remodel apartments to make them suitable for the elderly. Also, families may need to decide the degree to which they are willing to shoulder costs if renovating an apartment is a better decision for an older person than moving.

Group Living. One of the types of group living consists of subsidized apartments in a *senior complex.* Arrangements of this type can be run by cities, profit-making groups, or nonprofit agencies (including religious organizations). Many such projects were funded by the U.S. government through HUD (Department of Housing and Urban Development), which has stipulated that older persons can only be charged a certain percentage (e.g., 25 percent) of their income on rental. Senior housing usually requires that the older person be self-sufficient. Some complexes have organized social activities and health care on site. Others have mandatory meals served in a common area. In a given town, there may be several complexes, each run by an entirely different organization.

Another option of this type is the *group home,* in which several older persons live in a household where meals are served and laundry and other household chores are done, but little supervision or structured activities are provided. Group homes may or may not be licensed and/or regulated, depending on state rules.

Life-Care and Retirement Housing. One of the growing types of living arrangement is the *life-care facility,* in which an older person "buys" a unit (usually an apartment), lives independently, is served meals, and has a "guarantee" of care in a nursing home (often adjacent to the apartments) as part of the price of admission. This alternative is not, at present, tightly regulated, but it can be a useful choice for persons who can afford to protect themselves from the financial costs of long-term institutionalization.

Another growing area of housing alternatives for older persons with adequate financial resources is a *retirement community,* a planned community designed for older persons. There has been a substantial development of such communities in states with large elderly populations, such as California and Florida. However, they vary considerably in the facilities available and access to health care and other services, and are not subject to any particular regulation.

PURPOSES IN TALKING ABOUT HOUSING

One of the major purposes you will have in talking with your parents about housing should be to help them plan for changes they will need in either the immediate or distant future. One major problem in housing for the elderly is that the most desired options are frequently the least available; certain types of housing, such as subsidized apartments, have waiting lists of months and even years. Getting an older relative to put his or her name on a waiting list and fill out the appropriate paperwork can be arduous in that all of the issues—such as identity, loss, giving up the family home, and so forth—may have to be addressed first to "simply" prepare for events that may not even take place and, if they do, will take place in the future.

Another purpose may be driving home the reality that Mom or Dad cannot safely maintain herself or himself at home. Similarly, you may be in the position to drive home the fact that if Mom or Dad is to stay at home, some changes have to be made in the physical environment to accommodate to changes. This purpose frequently becomes urgent because of a crisis, such as a fall, a hospitalization, or some other emergency.

RESPONSES OF THE ELDERLY

An older person's residence has tremendous symbolic importance. Housing represents independence, access to services and/or transportation, the place in which a family has been raised, a link to others in a community, or a measure of one's status. When you suggest that older persons leave a setting that has so many meanings related to positive images of self, they may misinterpret the suggestion as a demand that they "give up" their identity and begin the "inevitable" slide to a nursing home. The fierceness with which some older persons hold on to their housing, despite its being too large, unsafe, or unmanageable, can be misinterpreted as their being stubborn, unrealistic, or rigid rather than their being concerned about independence, identity, and controlling their own environment.

Do not be surprised if your raising the issue of housing is greeted with some anxiety and related denial, anger, or disbelief by your parents. But remember, these reactions are frequently due to their own struggles to be independent, maintain themselves, and be in control of their environment. The idea of planning for a future move, as attractive as it seems, will be foreign to many parents and may be misinterpreted as you "hurrying them on" to an early demise.

On the other hand, your parents may greet your suggestions, *depending on how they are given*, with little resistance, especially if the suggestions tap into concerns they may have but are fearful of raising. The fear of raising the concerns, by the way, may come from feeling that the family will not listen, that their concerns are "foolish," that there are no alternatives except a nursing home, or that their concerns are the signs of a serious physical condition.

INFORMATION NEEDED

Making changes in housing takes careful preparation. One of the ways to be helpful to your parents is to do some initial research, even if it is only to find out where they can get information about a particular type of housing or housing situation. If you do too much work (e.g., by making contact with an agency or seeing an apartment) before even raising the issue with your parents, you could be viewed as meddling or trying to run their lives. However, getting some information as to what's available and where to find out more is a sensible minimum amount of preparation.

STEPS, STRATEGIES, TIME, AND TIMING

Sally, in her late forties, was the daughter of Lou Ella, 70. Lou Ella's husband had died in the last year. They had owned their own house, but Lou Ella was beginning to feel that the house was too big for her to handle alone. Sally thought Lou Ella wanted to be invited to live with her and her family. She felt guilty because she did not want her mother to live in their already overcrowded house, and would avoid discussing the topic with her mother or say things like "Oh, Mom, you can do it. Dad would want you to stay in the house."

Finally, after nine months of avoiding the topic, Sally decided she would have to tell her mother that there would be no room for her at her house. Fearing the worst, Sally waited until her mother made a comment about her own house being too big to run by herself. Then Sally asked, "Have you considered living someplace else?" Her mother replied, "Yes, I have considered moving into an apartment or senior housing, but I thought you wanted me to stay in the house where you were raised."

Sally was, of course, delighted and surprised at this outcome and was able to help her mother decide to put in an application for senior housing, which took another year to come to fruition.

This case highlights some of the issues steps and strategies to consider in talking with your parents about housing, although not all situations go as smoothly as things did for Sally and Lou Ella.

Emotional Preparation

On the emotional side, you should be prepared to handle your parents' likely reaction and the concerns that may underlie their negative feelings. To do so, you will have to avoid getting caught up in your own unresolved feelings about the issue (such as how bad Sally might have felt about her father's death), or you may inadvertently get pulled into the ties that keep your parents in undesirable living circumstances.

One related area to consider is the fears and myths your parent may have, such as "They want me to move in" (Lou Ella's concern), or "They really don't want me to move in," or "I cannot get along with X or Y," or "They don't really want to help me." Another consideration is fears or myths you may have, such as "She wants to move in and will not consider anything else" (which was Sally's concern) or "He won't listen," or "He doesn't care about what we think," or "She is stubborn, losing memory and intelligence, and is a typical old person." As I mentioned earlier, these myths will make things worse unless they are dispelled or addressed directly.

Another area is consideration for the older person's needs. What are, in actuality, the changes that suggest that a move is warranted? What are the older person's physical needs, needs for security, need for convenience and independence, need for access to desired activities, preferences for familiar surroundings or access to socialization for persons in his or her own age group? In Sally's situation, it was far better for her mother *not* to live with her.

In addition, be aware of the implications of decisions that will be made. Will there be guilt (on the part of either the older person or family members) because a choice is not wanted or fully agreed on? Will economic, time, or other resources be involved in ways that create undue or unmanageable stress?

Here are some guidelines for talking with your parents about housing:

- Know yourself and your parents. Know the best way to give them information so that it can be heard.
- Appreciate the role that their current housing has played for your parents: it represents personal territory, identity, a sense of independence and autonomy. Many moves come as a result of adaptation to losses, the move representing the physical giving up of prestige, power, and so forth.

- However you do it, have your parents be a critical part of the process from the beginning. People are more likely to follow through on decisions in which they have a part than on ones made for them. Encourage a frank discussion of wishes and preferences. (Notice that Sally used a question focusing on living options that opened the door for her mother to become an active decision maker).

- Appreciate that there are several roles you can play, ranging from detective (finding out about options) to sounding board, from judge to landlord. Some may be necessary to play, although at times, either you or your parent may not want you to play these roles.

- As much as you can, directly air your specific feelings about how you are working together.

- Decisions are not usually made suddenly and once and for all. Allow time (this may mean weeks or months) to sort out and decide, for both you and your parents.

- Present information rather than conclusions to your parents. With some prior approval, you can serve a good function by being a diligent detective rather than a judge and jury.

- Expect emotional reactions from both yourself and your parents. Some will have to do with acknowledging current and previous losses, some will be mourning the loss of housing lived in for many years. Emotional reactions are likely to surface indirectly—for example, in giving the movers a hard time, worrying too much about what to do with excess belongings, complaining about the new housing at the beginning (although some of the complaints might be justified).

- Above all, be prepared to talk and listen. There may be feelings about being a "good parent" or "good child" that enter into the decision (usually coupled with understandable but unnecessary concerns about hurting others' feelings) that get in the way of making appropriate decisions. You are all adults making decisions as to how one member will be living for a given period of time. Sorting them out makes sense so that they do not unnecessarily affect the series of decisions to be made about housing.

- Finally, get involved in learning and discussing housing options before a crisis occurs.

THEN WHAT?

Assuming you have begun your discussion about the need for some change, depending upon the interest, sophistication, and knowledge of your parents, you will, in all likelihood, need to gather or help gather more information. Talking about housing is only the first step. The process of finding housing options or even information on how to improve physical environment is not always simple. Because types of housing are run by quite different agencies and businesses, even finding telephone numbers to call in the Yellow Pages can be frustrating. You would do well to call several places such as those listed at the end of this chapter and get all of their information. Also, be sure to ask what other types of housing for the elderly are available in your area. Finally, *The Older American's Guide to Housing and Living Arrangements* by Margaret Gold is probably the best guide on the subject. I encourage you to invest in it if talking about housing is an important agenda for you and your parents.

RESOURCES

The following resources can be found fairly easily and should help you in talking about housing with older parents.

Gold, M. *The Older American's Guide to Housing and Living Arrangements*. Mount Vernon, N.Y.: Consumer Union, 1986. This book is a comprehensive description of types of housing arrangements, looking at the pros and cons of each. It has useful checklists and addresses for many organizations involved in housing for the elderly.

Call or write these agencies for information on housing:

State department on aging
Local area agency on aging
City/town housing commission

Look in the Yellow Pages for "Housing Consultants" or "Information and Referral."
Local universities with gerontology centers may have names of people in your area who are knowledgeable about housing options, home safety, and chore services.

8

Talking about Social Matters

Older persons frequently live in a social world that is shrinking as friends and spouses die or activity level is limited by health or financial restraints. Families, acting in their roles as caregivers, can find themselves drawn into the social world of their parents and feel helpless or rejected when their parents do not respond positively to their attempts to help.

On the one hand, it is easy to become involved in your parents' social concerns. On the other, it may seem convenient to shrug your shoulders and say, "It's their problem, so we will stay out of it."

If you are like most families, you will find yourself in the middle of these two extremes, caught between a desire to be helpful and supportive to your parents and a sense of independence that says that they should solve their problems in these areas without you. Both pulls are sensible; neither should be ignored.

In social concerns, there is considerable latitude for the roles and subsequent purposes of your talking to your parents. This chapter focuses on four issues related to social functioning: retirement, marriage and marital relationships, socialization, and activities.

TALKING ABOUT RETIREMENT

Ralph has been a worker in a factory all of his adult years. He looked forward to retiring at age 65, when he could "kick back and take it easy." His wife, Mary, thought they would spend time on social activities and travel, but Ralph, in his second month of retirement, has pretty much hung around the house and is becoming a bit sad about missing his friends at work. Mary worries out loud to their daughter, Eileen, on the telephone, telling her that Ralph seems depressed and that he shouldn't have retired, because he is becoming troublesome and she doesn't know what to do.

Facts and Figures

Retirement means leaving a job or position one has occupied. For most men, there is a clear shift between working and nonworking status.

For women, especially those who have worked as homemakers, "retirement" is less of an obvious change in status; after all, household work continues forever. At the same time, there is a growing category of "displaced homemakers," women who have become widows or divorced, who are faced with the multiple problems of being single and unemployed, who can have a difficult time of it in old age.

Robert Atchley, a noted gerontological sociologist, talks about retirement as having several phases or stages:

- *Preretirement,* a time when the individual realizes that retirement is near and starts disengaging from his or her job and making plans if none were made to date.
- *Honeymoon,* when the individual has officially retired and initially "plays" or vacations (assuming there are adequate financial resources to do so).
- *Retirement routine,* in which the individual settles down to a regular set of activities.
- *Rest and relaxation,* a time of low activity which is quite different from the honeymoon phase and may last for several years before the level of activity increases to what it had been prior to retirement.
- *Disenchantment,* in which some people feel depressed, let down, aimless, and upset (a fairly rare condition).
- *Reorientation,* in which people going through a disenchantment state get themselves together and reorient themselves to new activities and friends.
- *Routine,* in which the changes due to retirement have been handled.
- *Termination,* a time in which being retired is irrelevant, in part because the individual takes on a new job or meaningful activity, becomes ill or incapacitated, or devotes his or her life to caring for another person who is infirm.

Family members should be relieved to hear that most people adjust to retirement without major difficulties, and, even if there are problems in adjusting to having no routine, loss of friends, and loss of status connected with a job, many people work their way out of these problems without major traumas. Ralph, whose situation was mentioned in the beginning of this section, may well be adjusting to retirement and could work his way through to some sort of retirement routine. At the point we left him, it is too early to tell whether or not he will become satisfied with being retired. Mary (as well as his children) could certainly talk to him about their concerns, but should also appreciate that it may take time for him to overcome his own reactions.

Purposes in Talking about Retirement

One of the best reasons for talking about retirement with your parents is to get them to plan for financial as well as social aspects of retirement. You also may need to talk to them about how you see yourself relating to them when they are retired, as that can influence their decisions about issues such as selling a house, moving to another state, or moving near you. Other conceivable purposes include your being a sounding board as to the appropriateness of retirement or your doing some scouting for information that your parents need. A final purpose is to legitimize any "phasing" your parents go through upon retirement, as well as keeping an eye open for unusual behavior that suggests that all is not going well.

Responses, Strategies, and Steps

The major emotional reaction your parent may have is avoidance: telling you to wait, there is plenty of time to plan, and so forth. If you are getting this type of response, you will have to decide whether to respect it as a choice or to try to move things along. If you choose the latter, you would do well to focus on the consequences of not planning, having specific issues to discuss, and focusing on getting your parents to make the commitment to do some planning.

If you are concerned about adaptation to retirement, it will, in all honesty, be difficult to determine whether your parents are adapting well and can work things through on their own. One thought in this area is to assess how your parents have adapted to other changes in their lives, and assume that they will cope in much the same way. If prior coping patterns are problematic, then some discussion may be warranted.

Any way you go at it, you will also do well to find out your parents' plans, wishes, and concerns before giving your opinions or advice. It may be that you are both concerned about the same issues and can work together to formulate appropriate retirement plans.

TALKING ABOUT MARRIAGE AND MARITAL RELATIONSHIPS

Celia is the daughter of Anna, a widow in her late seventies. Celia is not particularly close to her mother but is interested in her well-being. They go out for lunch every week. Celia knows that her mother has been dating and is curious about the man. She does not know how to raise the subject, however, and does not want to make her mother feel uncomfortable.

Christopher, a widower in his early eighties, has been viewed as a "lady's man" by his children (Leonard, Max, and Mollie), who have supported his dating since his wife died ten years ago. Christopher winters in Florida and spends the rest of the year visiting his children, who live throughout the East and Midwest. This winter, however, he announced that he has met a woman he wants to marry. The marriage will take place in two months. ("We can't afford to wait" was his comment when asked why he seemed in a rush.) Also, they will settle down year-round in Florida in a small apartment. Christopher also indicates that his wife-to-be, who has her own family, wants nothing to do with Christopher's family and will not encourage visitors or visits to their homes.

Lisa, a woman in her forties, is the daughter of Sam and the stepdaughter of Suzanne, Sam's second wife. Sam and Suzanne had married fifteen years earlier and live nearby. Their marital relationship has been rocky, in part because Sam sometimes flies into a rage at the drop of a hat. Suzanne frequently calls Lisa to complain about his temper. Lisa feels torn between loyalty to her father and respect for Suzanne, because she too had been the victim of her father's rage in the past.

Marriage is, in many ways, a sacred institution. While married people have the social freedom to discuss their relationship with others, they do not grant other persons, including their children, equal freedom to comment on their marriage. In addition, adult children often have unfinished business with their parents about how they have related to each other in the past, which can in turn heighten difficulties in talking about existing relationships (which is part of Lisa's dilemma) as well as future relationships (Christopher's and Celia's situations).

Facts and Figures

More than half of the elderly are married. Most elderly men are married (over 70 percent); most elderly women are not (only 36 percent are married). Remarriages in old age are also becoming more common. In 1976, for example, there were almost 50,000 marriages of persons age 65 or over, 95 percent of which were second marriages.

Most couples are happy with their marriages. The major changes that affect the older couple include retirement, not having children in the house, and increased reliance on each other for emotional and physical support. The most common type of support involves a husband who depends on a younger and healthier wife for physical aid if he is is ill or develops a disability.

Sexual activity, despite beliefs to the contrary, does not automatically stop when your parents reach the age you think they should stop it. Some studies of older couples suggest that the majority have sexual intercourse regularly and that, for many, sex is better than it was in earlier years. Even with the changes of menopause for women and fears about sexual failure for men (stemming from the fact that sexual stimulation takes longer for elderly males), most older couples consider sexual expression in all its forms an important part of their lives.

Purposes in Talking about Marriage

Your purposes in talking about your parents' marriage are multiple: to express opinions, to lay the cards on the table for your own sake, to attempt to separate yourself from your parents' difficulties, to try to get them to change their behavior toward each other, to "avoid harm" (such as not going into a second marriage or a divorce), or to get them to go for professional help for concerns in their relationship, including counseling for sexually related issues. You may have specific concerns, such as the importance of prenuptial agreements before a second marriage takes place, confronting your parents when you feel one is not taking satisfactory care of the other as a caregiver, or specific requests for contact (all of which could be concerns for Christopher's children). However, your role should not be that of a marriage counselor. It is too easy to become drawn into problems that are rightfully your parents' business and become, even with the best of intentions, the third leg of a triangle in which all members are defensive, play games with each other, and feel miserable (like Lisa in the example at the beginning of this section).

Responses of the Elderly

You are likely to get a range of responses when you talk about marriage with your parents. Inasmuch as the issues you address are sensitive, there may be some (understandable) defensiveness when they are raised. At the same time, just because you are being greeted with open arms does not mean that you are being understood. It is also possible to be misconstrued as being an ally against another person (spouse or potential spouse) when you are, in fact, attempting to be neutral in a marital situation, such as Lisa's situation with Suzanne. At the same time, some parents may welcome honest concern and inquiry into their affairs. For example, if Celia (the daughter who takes her mother to lunch weekly) could handle her uncertainty, Anna might welcome her daughter's support of her becoming intimate with a man.

Information Needed

Depending on the situation and your purpose, you can need a range of information in preparation for the discussion. If, for example, you are concerned that others may exploit your parent, you will need to know how to protect your parent's rights legally. You may have to consult a lawyer or other legal authority to be sure about the laws of the state regarding, among other issues, prenuptial agreements. If you are more concerned about the relationship, you should have the names of persons who are both competent and interested in the elderly that you may refer your parents to. If you are concerned about issues related to sexuality, you may need the names of professionals who handle problems related to sexual functioning, such as certified sex therapists. If you are dealing more with who visits whom, limit setting, or clearing the air, you may worry less about information matters than about how to handle the overriding emotional issues that are at the heart of your discussion.

Steps, Strategies, Time, and Timing

Each major discussion about marital issues is likely to include unfinished business or unresolved issues from the past. For example, both Lisa's and Christopher's children's discussions with their parents will be tinged with feelings about previous spouses. Even Celia, who, at the beginning of this chapter, simply wants to talk with Anna about her boyfriend, can be stuck because of mixed feelings about her mother "betraying" the memory of her father. Other family members are going to be highly involved, either immediately or when the dust settles. You would do well to attempt initially, on your own (or with help from a counselor, a sensitive spouse, or significant others, including your children), to sort out the different threads of your concerns and figure out which need to be addressed, which you need to put aside, and then how to address each concern.

Assuming that you have your various agendas sorted out, consider the following points in developing a strategy for discussing your concerns about your parents' marriage:

- Appreciate their sense of failure that may come from having you raise the topic.
- Go in with the hope of succeeding.
- Be particularly careful to use "I" language.
- Allow time for your parents to experience pain and emotional reactions to what you are saying *before* you get into any specific requests for action on their part.
- If you have requests (for time, for visits, for them *not* to talk to you in ways that create triangulation, for example), be prepared to make them in small steps and *slowly*, with lots of opportunity to discuss the steps as well as react emotionally to them.
- Ask open-ended questions, and *listen* to their responses.
- Be congruent and empathic, and keep your sense of being an individual intact.
- Have a fall-back plan open to maintain contact no matter what is said and done (e.g., agree at the beginning that you will call on the phone in two weeks to "see how things are going").
- If the situation is one in which you have serious concerns about your parent's welfare (as Christopher's children do), you should be prepared to be assertive and, at the same time, point out that your concerns are out of love and compassion and that you are going to maintain contact even though what you are talking about is painful for all of you.

Outcomes

One of the things I suggest for those of you brave enough to talk to your parents about their marriage is to set limited goals for outcomes. Changes will take time to surface. Many issues will be involved in your discussions, in spite of your careful sorting out of issues beforehand. You should give yourself a mental pat on the back for addressing the issue—even more so if, afterward, you decide you did it fairly cleanly. At the same time, if you decide to not address it for healthy reasons (i.e., if your sense of self-esteem is high for choosing to leave matters alone), you can also give yourself a pat.

The issues and concerns about marital relationships are difficult. It is hard to tell your parent who is getting married to someone you do not trust that you are concerned and saddened about matters of inheritance when your words may be perceived as greed or a statement about your parent's happiness. It is painful to listen to your mother tell you how she has put up with your father for many years and wants to get divorced. It is hard to fight the loss of contact when your parent goes along with a new spouse's preference to spend severely limited time with you. It is equally hard to imply that one of your parents (or stepparents) is not taking care of the other, especially if the other is placating or otherwise going along with things. As long as you do *not* make either you or your parent feel you have to be totally content with the outcome for it to work, then you can live with pain, with difficult situations, and keep the possibilities of talking about things open. That will be the most important outcome you can have in many of these situations.

What Needs to Be Said, What You Can Live with Saying

As is true for other aspects of talking to your parents about marriage, this depends primarily on you. Unless there will be some obvious harm to your parent as a result of your being silent, you have to decide what is important *for your own sense of self-esteem* to say as the "bottom line." The rest will be a function of how well things are going, how well you are all listening, and how difficult the issues to be discussed are for all of you.

TALKING ABOUT SOCIALIZING

Arlene, the daughter of Jenny, 65, called a local social service agency to ask for help. "My mother is having a problem. My father died unexpectedly six months ago after being retired only a few months. My mother had expected to spend her retirement years with him, traveling and enjoying their hobbies and friends. It has been six months since the death, and she should be finished grieving. Can you get her involved in activities?" When asked if she had discussed the issue with her mother, Arlene seem a bit flustered, saying, "I couldn't do that." Subsequent counseling led to Arlene's realization of her fear that if she began the process with her mother, she would become so involved that she would never become disengaged. With professional help, Arlene was eventually able to raise the topic with her mother and to encourage her to go out, without feeling that she had to make sure that her mother did so. Jenny did, in fact, join a senior club and became an occasional participant in activities.

Sandy, in her forties, was concerned about her husband's aunt Elizabeth, a woman in her late seventies who had never married and had lived a solitary life in Dallas. Sandy was forever asking Elizabeth to go to the local senior center, join clubs, have visitors, and do other worthwhile activities, all of which Elizabeth steadfastly refused. Finally, after several go-rounds, Sandy accepted Elizabeth's refusals as legitimate and felt that she had discharged her sense of obligation by making the offers, even if they were refused.

Issues and Facts

Most older persons are not socially isolated. Their major source of social support, however, is the family. In part this is because many older people are single. In our culture, most socializing takes place among people of the same age, with couples being the "normal" unit for social activity. A single older person is somewhat excluded from many ordinary social interactions unless she (or, less frequently, he) makes a special effort to go against custom.

At the same time, the preponderance of single elderly persons (mostly widows) and concerns about their social life have led to creation of programs designed to promote socializing, such as senior citizen centers, congregate meal sites, and social clubs in senior housing. But these organizations do not meet the needs of all elderly. Programs that have been around for any length of time may have a group of members who have been there for a considerable amount of years together that will seem intimidating to a "new" person. Also, the range of ages among senior citizens can vary by as much as thirty years. Activities for older persons may be an answer to needs for socializing; then again, they may not.

Another issue regarding social activities has to do with the multiple pulls on younger families as they take on varying degrees of responsibility for their elders' social life. Because of work demands, children's schedules, and the desire for independence, you may not want to include your mother or father in every social event. At the same time, there are countless families who feel guilt over leaving their parents alone on a weekend while they go out to enjoy themselves.

Responses of the Elderly

Socializing fulfills several needs for older persons. One is to provide meaningful interaction, activities, and a sense of purpose. Another is to provide a degree of intimacy, an opportunity to have others to talk with and relate to. A third is to promote better health and a sense of well-being.

All of these are valuable goals. The problem is that there may be individual choices, individual fears, lack of appropriate options, and beliefs (about a stigma associated with a program, about the family providing social life, and so forth) that can interfere with an older person's getting involved or staying active. Some older persons, like Elizabeth in the example above, are probably better off (or at least can be viewed as making a clear choice) not getting involved. Others may need considerable encouragement and working through family and individual issues before changes can be made in social activities.

How involved should families be in the social needs of elderly members? Like Arlene, some family members are afraid that their involvement will become a long-standing obligation that they do not want. In addition, some older persons implicitly expect that the family will be their sole social support and that having to go elsewhere for their activities is a sign of failure, showing that the family does not love them fully or that they are unworthy of love. Part of this concern may come from what was usual in your parents' generation as they grew up (a "generational value"). Part may be due to fears about going to new places and entering social situations that will be awkward at first.

In order to attempt to overcome these difficulties, you will have to figure out which are operating in your particular situation and how to lessen their impact as best you can. If the problem is your own fear of getting overinvolved, you would do well to set some limits in your own mind (as well as with your parent) at the beginning, rather than make promises you cannot keep. Also, you would do well to have linkages to the senior center, group activity, or desired program from the start that will help you disengage to the degree that is appropriate for you, your parent, and the context in which you find yourselves.

If your parent believes that the family does not love him or her, the only way you are going to overcome this hurdle is to talk about it, directly and clearly, *without* guilt or blame. You will have to be encouraging and reassuring, as well as continually answering questions or concerns from your parent that stem from the question of "who loves whom."

If the problem is a generational norm, then the issues are a bit different. Your parent could change her or his view if appropriate information is received—for example, from others who share your parent's beliefs about families, seem content with their family relationships, and participate in activities outside of the family. (It will be of help if these people, whom you may be able to call in to talk with your parent, are people your parent respects and feels comfortable socializing with.) Even in this case, however, you will do well to talk directly with your parent about what you are doing and why you are doing it.

Information Needed

If you are to embark on a "socialization" mission for your parent, you ought to know what the options are and how to make contact if your parent decides to take part in activities. While there are a range of programs for the elderly in any city, usually there is some sort of department for the aged in the Yellow Pages (or its blue, green, or orange cousins of municipal listings) that you can consult for an information and referral agency. Be careful not to do your parents' work for them, but at the same time try to get enough information to know what is possible, including arrangements for transportation, meals, and the hours a program is open.

A second area that can satisfy needs for both social contact and meaningful activity is volunteering. There are numerous volunteer programs in most communities, some of which are listed at the end of this chapter.

Some initial research will ease a connection if your parent agrees to go ahead on the matter.

An additional way to promote socializing is on a paid job. While only about 15 percent of older persons are in the work force, there are many who might work if they found the right part-time job. Your information-hunting mission in this case includes finding out where the jobs are, what the time aspects are, and, most important, how much your parent can work without losing benefits such as Social Security. Calls to the Social Security office or an information and referral telephone system should also get you the information you need in this area.

Steps, Strategies, Time, and Timing

Several important issues have already been raised as to how to go about talking to your parents about socializing:

- Pick your fights carefully. That is, you need to start with a step in the right direction as your focus of discussion.
- Be specific, not general. It will be much easier to say, for example, "I want you to visit the senior center one time to see what it is like," rather than, "You should go to a senior center; it will be good for you." Volunteering is a bit easier to push since it entails doing for others, thus offering reciprocal relationships. But even here, a specific request, such as "I want you to call up and find out what the volunteer program is about," is easier for your parents to hear than "You should become a volunteer."
- Consider your timing. It is better not to recommend a new activity while your parent is feeling really down about something and does not have the energy to do anything. Instead, wait until there seems to be enough energy to act on a suggestion. Similarly, making a suggestion during the holiday season about seeking social contact may convey the idea that you do not want your parent around at this time of year when families usually get together. To push the point a bit, recommending that your parents go out to a new place at a time when the weather is bad may lead to a rational refusal to venture forth into the elements. Finally, give your parents time to consider what you have said so that the decision is, in fact, theirs to take the first step in socializing. This means that you need to have patience and let your parents set the pace of change.

- Pay attention to *how* you explain your purpose. Realize that when you try to get your parents to interact with others, they may think you are turning away from them or telling them how to live their lives. You therefore must consider carefully what you say to set the stage for your discussion. My preference is to start by finding common ground on which there is agreement, such as the fact that your parent feels there is nothing to do or feels lonely, and then move on to posing the situation as a problem that you both have to solve.
- Prepare other family members to support your efforts.
- Include your parents in the decision process. Unless they are involved in making decisions about what to do, you will be doing their work for them (and they may act to sabotage your efforts).

Outcomes

You may have to live with limited outcomes of your efforts to expand your parents' social life. At the same time, you need to have some immediate, short-term first steps in mind as signs that movement is being made. People's social lives are their own business. Our role with our parents is not to be intrusive, but rather to give them options and help them handle the fear, anxiety, or other feelings behind their reluctance to socialize. The boundary between being helpful and meddling in this area is perhaps the least clear of all areas in this book.

What You Can Live with Saying

Again, you have to decide how much you want to tell your parents about your feelings about their activities and how much you are simply talking with them for their sake. That decision will determine what you can live with saying. It is not, however, always an easy decision to make.

RESOURCES

Atchley, R. C. *Social Forces and Aging: An Introduction to Social Gerontology.* 4th ed. Belmont, Calif.: Wadsworth Publishing Co., 1985. This is a college textbook, one of the best for an overview of aging, including social issues and policy concerns.

Brecher, E. M. *Love, Sex, and Aging, a Consumer's Union Report.* Mount Vernon, N.Y.: Consumers Union, 1984. This report discusses sexual behavior and attitudes of over 400 persons over the age of 50 who answered a survey administered by Consumers

Union on topics related to love and sex. It gives valuable insights into expected changes and behavior from the older population on these topics.

Butler, R., and M. I. Lewis. *Sex after Sixty: A Guide for Men and Women in Their Later Years*. New York: Harper & Row, 1976. Written by two preeminent figures in mental health and aging, this book clearly spells out myths and facts about sexuality and old age.

Hooyman, N. R., and W. Lustbader. *Taking Care: Supporting Older People and Their Families*. New York: Free Press, 1986. This is another excellent guide for families in handling the problems of older relatives.

Porcino, J. *Growing Older, Getting Better: A Handbook for Women in the Second Half of Life*. Reading, Mass.: Addison-Wesley, 1983. This book addresses a wide range of issues and concerns of older women, including those addressed in this chapter.

Silverstone, B., and H. K. Hyman. *You and Your Aging Parent*. Mount Vernon, N.Y.: Consumers Union, 1982. One of the best guides for family members in dealing with an older person's problems.

Many communities have senior citizen centers, run by municipalities, churches, or other organizations. Consult your local telephone book to find ones near you. They may be listed in the Yellow Pages under aging services or social service agencies.

ACTION is the federal organization responsible for RSVP (Retired Senior Volunteers Program) and other federally run volunteer programs. Their address is 806 Connecticut Avenue, NW, Washington, DC 20525. Their toll-free number is (800) 424-8580.

There are also many other volunteer opportunities in communities, including tutoring programs in public schools, hospital groups, and fraternal organizations. Your local United Way or Area Agency on Aging may be a good source of lists of volunteering opportunities.

Some communities have job placement bureaus for older persons, which may be run by a municipality or state-based organizations.

The American Association of Retired Persons is the largest organization of older adults in the country. It advocates programs for the elderly, offers discounts for seniors on trips and services, and makes available or publishes newsletters and other publications. AARP has local chapters that meet regularly. The national headquarters are at 1909 K Street, NW, Washington, DC 20049. Telephone: (202) 872-4700.

9

Talking about Legal and Financial Matters

Linda was 68 when she had a stroke that left her without speech and with difficulty writing. At that time, her family thought it would be wise to have legal access to her bank accounts "in case anything happened." Unfortunately, her daughter, Sara, did not feel she should talk about such things with her mother and that the discussion would make her mother feel they were giving up on her.

Two years later, Linda began to show signs of Alzheimer's disease. As the family was wondering what to do about her assets, which included a house in a wealthy suburb, Linda had another stroke. After three weeks in the hospital, she had to go to a nursing home. She was barely conscious and could not sign her name. Without intervention through the courts, there was no immediate way for Linda's bills to be paid, except by her children, who had to take out a bank loan to do it.

Bessie was a proper woman in her nineties. She had been raised in a family of great wealth during the early 1900s, but the wealth had been lost during the Great Depression. While in her eighties she had developed a series of medical problems that meant that she needed a live-in companion. Her three children, Tyler, Richard, and Stella, decided that they would tell their mother to pay a certain amount per month, which was within her budget, for the live-in help, but that they would quietly subsidize the rest of the financial burden to assure their mother of having live-in care while she needed it. Bessie died at 94. There were no regrets in the family about the silent bargain that had been struck.

These two cases represent only a few of the situations of the elderly that become entangled when legal and financial crises strike. How families talk about these issues is critical in both planning for crises and responding to them when they occur. In Linda's case, the family probably erred in not making arrangements ahead of time. However, for them to plan ahead with Linda would have required substantial reassurance that they were not giving up on her. At the same time, in Bessie's case, the family decision to support her silently while she paid some of the bill, without including her in the decision, could hardly be faulted.

Legal and financial matters are difficult to talk about. One reason is that most legal and financial concerns of children are based on uncertainty, either relating to *whether* the plan will go into effect (such as a trust fund to be used if an older relative becomes incapacitated) or *when* (such as a will). At the same time, going through the planning process can raise any fears your parent has about the underlying issue, whether it is incapacitation, institutionalization, or dying. These fears and concerns are unpleasant enough to stop the planning process.

In addition, little of the benefit of talking about these issues will accrue directly to the person making legal or financial decisions, especially those related to wills, trusts, and estates. The exceptions are, of course, talking with the elderly about benefits to which they are entitled and preventing from them losing assets to con artists. About the best we can do is point out the hardships that will fall on the rest of us, including spouses, children, and grandchildren, if plans are not made in advance. However, if there are hard feelings to begin with, if there is low trust or low self-esteem, I will tell you outright that talking about these matters will raise suspicions about motives and you will be in for some nasty exchanges.

Even if there are good feelings on all sides, it will still be difficult to discuss the topic. As one expert in the field put it, "There is *no* good way to tell older people they are not handling their finances adequately." Luckily for our purposes, he also agreed that while there was no perfect way to do it, some ways are better than others, and that children can decide what they will and will not talk about. The key point is that you can minimize guilt and frustration by dealing directly with these matters *or* choosing to not deal with them and realizing the emotional and financial price that you may pay thereby. Also, you can appreciate that even if things do not work out for the best, you have made the soundest choices possible for yourself and your parents.

FACTS AND DEFINITIONS

For many of us, the most pressing legal matters regarding our elderly relatives come in to our awareness too late, as happened with Linda and Sara. It is sad to delay taking action until a parent is incapacitated and we cannot get to their assets to pay for their care, or when older people become paupers because medical and nursing home fees deplete their assets, or when a will is found to be incomplete (or never drawn up), meaning endless headaches with courts, or when the family is left without any indication of the wishes of an older relative who is too ill to communicate with the rest of the family.

Many legal and financial plans and agreements are available for families to use in either planning or reacting to situations in which the capacity of their older relative is severely diminished. Some of the most common ones as well as some common entitlement programs are defined below.

Governmental Programs

Social Security. Social Security, which was part of legislation enacted in 1935, was intended to guarantee older persons a certain amount of *supplemental* income in old age. It was billed as an "insurance" program, but, in actuality, the income received from Social Security is dispensed immediately, and people who retired in the first few decades of Social Security's existence received far more dollars than they put into the program. Eligibility for Social Security depends on the type of job one has had (or one's spouse has had). The amount of money allocated each month is determined by formulas that take into account years worked and money earned in given years. Although the age for retirement has been 65, with some people opting for earlier retirement for a decreased benefit rate, the Reagan administration has proposed raising the retirement age to 68 in the year 2002.

Supplemental Security Income (SSI). Supplementary Security Income was a program designed for the poor elderly. It is a supplement to Social Security that ensures a minimal guaranteed income. States may also supplement federal subsidies in this area, but to be on SSI one has to have a detailed examination of all assets, called a "means test."

Medicare. This is a federally run health insurance program for the elderly. One is eligible for the program by virtue of being eligible for Social Security. Part A includes in-patient hospital expenses, certain home health care, and fairly limited parts of nursing home care. Part B, which requires a monthly payment by the older person and is voluntary, includes some physician and out-patient services.

Medicaid. This program is designed to be comprehensive and is available only for "indigent" persons (those who cannot pay for their health care). Each state has its own Medicaid system, which is funded in part by state and federal governments. Eligibility is determined by each state.

Nursing home care and hospital care are included; some states include home care, prescription drugs, dental care, and mental health services, although the rate of reimbursement to participating providers is so low as to make many of them unwilling to take on Medicaid patients in great numbers. In certain states there is a residency requirement, which can make it hard for people who lived in the state for many years, retired to another state, and then returned so as to be near family and familiar resources in a time of severe health or other problems.

Other Programs. Other programs exist for older persons in various states and communities, such as tax breaks on homes, fuel assistance, discounts at stores, and decreases in fares in public transportation. Each program is likely to have different criteria for eligibility (age, income, or need) and needs to be researched with the appropriate sponsoring agency.

Administrative Appeals Procedures. In all federal and state benefits programs, families and older persons should be aware that there are administrative appeals procedures by which they can challenge decisions by agencies as to eligibility or whether they will pay.

Legal Options

The following options are available in practically all states (the one exception being living wills, which are not as universal as other options), although their form and method of use will vary.

Power of Attorney. This term indicates that one person (e.g., your parent) has given full consent to have another person carry out his or her instructions in limited or even in all financial matters. Power of attorney can be made "durable" so that it stays in effect even if your parent becomes incapacitated. It may be "springing" in that it would only go into effect in the event that your parent becomes unable to make decisions independently. Although a range of forms to designate a person as having power of attorney are available, it is prudent to use forms from your own bank or financial institution.

Representative Payee. This term refers to a provision of Social Security and several other benefits packages by which a person other than the incapacitated older person can receive monthly retirement checks but has to use them for the older person's living expenses. This is accomplished by applying to the appropriate paying agency.

Trusts. A trust is a legal arrangement by which an individual designates others to manage certain funds according to his or her instructions. Much like power of attorney, trusts can be developed to become active only upon the incapacity of an individual. Trusts are also used in distributing inheritance to provide limited access to assets for individuals, usually children. Trusts need to be drawn up with attorneys. Care has to be taken to make sure that the trustees will act in the best interests of the person for whom the trust is established.

Competency. This term means that an individual is capable of making decisions and managing his or her affairs. A person is considered competent until proven otherwise—and to prove incompetency can mean considerable money and time spent in the courts; often the outcome hangs on the decision of a judge. This can be difficult, especially when an older person is alert and gregarious but also quite confused.

Conservatorship. A conservator is someone who has legal responsibility either for financial/asset control (conservatorship of estate) or for the total legal decisions for an individual (conservatorship of person). The latter would include decisions about institutionalization, medical care, and so forth. Conservatorship must be accomplished through a petitioning of the courts, which have the power to appoint whomever they see fit to manage the affairs of the individual. At the same time, if there has been prior inclusion of the older person in the process (or even naming a proposed conservator in one's will), the likelihood that an appropriate person will be named as conservator is increased.

Joint Financial Accounts. Most financial vehicles, including bank accounts, money market accounts, stocks, and bonds, can be put in "joint" ownership, with any of the owners having access to the account or stock. Provided there is trust between the people involved, having joint accounts makes getting to assets easier in the event of incapacity without taking assets away from an individual. Joint ownership may raise issues of taxation liability, so one should consult with an accountant or appropriate lawyer before moving in this direction.

Gifts. As of 1986, individuals can give up to $10,000 to any individual in any given year without paying any "gift" tax (therefore avoiding inheritance tax, as the assets are being given before one is deceased). Each partner in a marriage may give $10,000 to anyone he or she chooses. The person receiving the money is then responsible for paying taxes on any money the gift earns for them.

Will. A will is a legal document that specifies how you wish your assets to be distributed upon your death. It may include provisions for trusts;

usually names an executor, or individual who will oversee the distribution of assets; and can list contingencies such as who will be executor if the named executor is unable to fulfill that obligation. Although it entails some money and time to draw up a will, these costs are far less than the court costs to the estate if no will is made. Having a will is one of the most important things an individual can do to ensure that his or her wishes are fulfilled after death.

It can be hard to bring up the subject of wills with an aging parent, as it brings with it a recognition that the parent will die and is, in essence, like asking the older person to confront his or her mortality, however painful it may be, primarily for the benefit of potential survivors. It is also possible that the one who raises the issue may be seen as "greedy" by other family members.

Living Will. The living will is recognized in some states as a legal indication of what dramatic life-sustaining measures an individual may or may not want to be taken in case of incapacitation or severe illness. Living will legislation has been passed by some states, although the existence of such a will usually means that several people, including physicians, clergy, and family members, have to decide when the living will is operative and what measures are considered dramatic or extraordinary. The reason for having such a document is to spare an individual from physical suffering her or she does not want, or, secondarily, to preserve assets from being spent fruitlessly to maintain life at all costs when there may be little advantage in so doing. Living wills are one way to handle the legal, medical, and ethical issues about the cost of health care in the last days or months of an individual's life.

PURPOSES IN TALKING ABOUT LEGAL AND FINANCIAL MATTERS

There are several varied purposes in talking about legal and financial matters with your parents. It is wise to consider your purpose carefully as a first step in formulating how you are going to discuss matters.

Planning (Warding Off Harm)

One important purpose of having discussions about these matters is to help your parent plan for future possibilities or, in the case of making a will, eventualities. Advance planning is advisable because it enables people to think things over at a time when there is no immediate crisis, and topics can be raised to open the door for further discussions at a later date.

The ease of planning will depend to a large extent on the ease of comfort in the relationship you have with your parent. If we ever need a reason other than psychological well-being to be on good terms with older relatives, having enough trust to make sensible financial plans is a good one.

Avoiding Fraud (Warding Off Harm)

It is not uncommon to read in the newspaper about confidence games that trick older people into withdrawing their savings and giving them to bogus bank examiners or people who claim to have found money and persuade the older person to put up "trust" money to ensure that they will share in a recovery fee. Older persons need to know that phony credentials can be obtained, telephone numbers can be found out, and any promise of a big "find" is probably not one at all. Your role as a family member is to make sure that your communication and relationship are good enough that you would be consulted before any major transaction of this type takes place.

Education

Most people do not understand all the terms and arrangements for financial and legal issues, so there is a need for some education as to what is meant, implied, or otherwise indicated by taking various legal steps. Thus, one purpose of talking with your parents about legal matters is to help them become educated about these options so that they are making the best choices they can. Education can take place through direct discussion (raising a topic and then finding out more) or indirectly (e.g., giving your parents this chapter or other materials to read and then discussing parts of it with them to decide what needs to be pursued further).

Exploring Soft Signs of Trouble

At times, you may wonder if all is well with your parents' finances— whether they have enough to get by, are still able to manage, and so forth. In these cases, you will need to find out more information from them, sometimes subtly, at other times more directly.

> Caroline, in her mid-eighties, had been a homemaker all of her married life but had, along with her husband, carefully saved for her old age. Her two grandchildren, Matty and Sue, were in their mid-thirties with children of their own. Caroline continually embarrassed the grand-children, not to mention her daughter, Evaline, by giving them what seemed to be too-large gifts (like $200 for a birthday for one of the children). The family tried "everything," like not reminding Grandma that it was the kids' birthday or threatening to give the money away. Once they even bought Caroline a dress worth the exact value of the gift; they took the tag off of the dress, which Caroline promptly gave away to the local Salvation Army.
>
> At the end of their rope, Matty and her husband finally developed a communication strategy that would resolve matters. One day, they sat down with Caroline and talked with her. "Grandma," Matty said, "we do not like getting these gifts for all this money. It seems like you are spending too much money on us and not enough on yourself."
>
> They waited with bated breath for her answer. "Don't you young people understand?" she asked. "You should know that there're taxes to be paid if all this money is in my accounts when I'm gone."

Matty and her husband left the discussion feeling much better about the gifts, which continued. By directly addressing the issue, they finally realized that this was Caroline's way of distributing her estate without waiting for her will to go into effect. (They also, fortunately, had good enough relationships with other family members that everyone soon realized the reasons for Caroline's behavior.)

Soft signs of trouble with finances can include failure to pay bills or continued mistakes in a checkbook that was formerly kept accurately. If you find signs that your parent is having trouble handling finances, you need to figure out the extent of potential damage and how to talk about it with your parent to ward off harm. This will not be easy, as you may well be met with denial and avoidance.

At the same time, if you feel that changes need to be made, you should be prepared to be assertive, direct, and willing to listen to your parent's fears and concerns, which may come out in the form of anger, ration-alization, or denial. Unless you are prepared to take specific legal actions to forcibly control your parent's assets, your parent has to have control over decisions and needs to be able to make up his or her own mind about any changes in how financial matters are handled.

There will be times when you will want your parents to make a specific decision or action, such as making out a will, signing for power of attorney, applying for an entitlement, or appealing a decision on Medicare or Social Security. There will be specific outcomes associated with this purpose. If there is no crisis, it is a good idea to think of a series of steps that you can take to get to the overall goal. Foremost in your thinking, however, should be the realization that you will be asking your parents to make a decision that leads to others having more control over their resources. It is crucial that your parents be included in the decision as early as possible and that the decision be "theirs."

Responding to a Crisis

One of the occasions for talking about legal and related matters is when there has been a sudden and perhaps dramatic change in functioning that warrants discussion. At the same time, what appears to be a crisis (such as hospitalization or institutionalization) may not mean that your parent has to give up total control of legal and personal matters. Your communication and relationship will have a strong bearing on how much uncertainty you can put up with as a trade-off for your parent's sense of control and identity by handling financial matters.

> Alvin, a widower aged 85, was the patriarch of his family. He was well off, a retired accountant. He viewed his children, especially his son, Mark, as needing his advice in financial matters. At the same time, Alvin had a heart condition and diabetes, and he had made some bad investments in stocks. Mark began to worry about his father's managing his finances but felt that if he talked about it with him, his father would not listen.
>
> Alvin eventually had a fall that led to his being placed in a nursing home. While he retained control of his mental faculties, he began to rely on his son to carry out his financial wishes. After a while Alvin allowed Mark to carry out financial plans that *Mark* had decided were necessary. These changes were sufficient to decrease Mark's concerns. He was also happy to allow his father to maintain "control" over his finances.

Although Alvin had full legal control over his finances, the change in his living situation and Mark's willingness to let his father have control over his decisions made things better from Mark's point of view. While there were no legal changes to give Mark power of attorney, he felt comfortable with things the way they were and also felt that taking any more control away from his father (e.g., taking power of attorney) was not worth the negative reaction he felt his father would have if the topic were raised.

RESPONSES OF THE ELDERLY AND THE FAMILY

Your emotional responses and those of your elderly parents and the rest of the family to legal and financial issues are likely to be representative of every conflict, connection, norm, and value your family has. Money, assets, and control over decisions symbolize any and all of the following: power, control, identity, ability to influence others, dominance, the nature of relationships, and self-indulgence. Any discussion of these topics can trigger the feelings related to them. The feelings may not surface directly, but may lend heat to the discussion and topics being discussed.

Your family probably already has rules and norms about money, including what can and cannot be discussed, who is in charge of what, who can raise issues, who has to be included or excluded in discussions, and so forth. The only way I know to change the rules safely is to discuss them with the appropriate parties. Specific requests can alter unspoken rules, but they have to be made directly and carefully.

Many of the discussions you will have will absolutely mean that your parent is giving some control over assets away. There may be grief, anger, frustration, and fear associated with these actions. To deny this reality will be destructive in the long run. It is also not useful to be falsely reassuring (such as saying, "Don't worry, Dad, you're still in control"), especially when your parents are feeling that control is lost. The reminder as to what they are in control of will be useful, but later, after the emotional reaction surfaces and is expressed.

Loss of control is also one of the great unspoken fears of older persons who face giving up some decision-making power over their lives. Expect that your parents may have worries and concerns that existed before you began this discussion and that they are also as concerned as you are about how assets will be distributed and what happens if they become incapacitated. As was said earlier, your previous and current relationship will determine how much you can discuss these issues.

INFORMATION NEEDED

Legal and financial matters are ones about which you will need significant information and advice before you take specific steps. Consult with an attorney who is familiar with these matters, a legal aid society, or a public interest law firm that focuses on needs of the elderly to find out what the specific legal issues are for your particular situation.

Finding information can be difficult. You would do well to read specific statutes or know that you are trusting an attorney to give you correct advice the same way your parents have to trust you if you are becoming legally involved in the control of their assets.

Finally, you will need to keep abreast of new legislation that may touch on power of attorney, conservatorship, wills, and other issues related to your individual concerns.

STEPS, STRATEGIES, TIME, AND TIMING

Even though the range of concerns relating to legal and financial matters is wide, certain guidelines from other places in this book can be of assistance to you:

• Start your discussions early, before a crisis arises, even though your discussions may only be successful in raising topics.

• Listen carefully to your parents' concerns. If possible, do not react in an escalating way when they voice their fears.

• Use "I" statements to talk about your concerns.

• Be prepared for projection and guilt on all parties' parts. Have fallback strategies to deescalate arguments that are specific and calmly put.

• Try to enlist other family members to help. An "outsider" (e.g., an in-law) may have an easier time talking about these matters than a son or daughter.

• Be prepared for a refusal to cooperate. If you are getting no cooperation, remember that, except for taking legal measures (such as applying for conservatorship), you need your parent to cooperate in all of these matters. When faced with refusal, try to leave the door open by acknowledging the disagreement but saying you would like to talk about these things again at a later time. You can also focus on looking at the consequences of actions taken (or not taken), find common points of agreement, and use other strategies and skills for handling difficult situations.

OUTCOMES, WHAT YOU HAVE TO SAY, WHAT YOU CAN LIVE WITH SAYING

The outcomes of your discussions, while depending on your purpose, will have implicit next steps in many cases. You will have to take care that difficulties in obtaining accurate information about entitlements, appeals, or legal actions do not become so discouraging to you or your parents that you take things out on each other. You need to carefully decide whether it is worth it to discuss matters or let things be and hope for the best. You should also try to make your decisions cleanly, that is, to know when you are taking a risk by not discussing matters, know when you are choosing to go ahead despite the possibility of hard feelings, and know, with a sense of high self-worth, that things may not work out for the best. With all of these in mind, you could come out of these difficult discussions minimizing guilt, mistakes in judgment, or other potential negative outcomes.

RESOURCES

The Social Security Administration, U.S. Department of Health, Education, and Welfare, can provide information about benefits, Medicare, and Medicaid.

The following pamphlets are available from the U.S. Government Printing Office, Superintendent of Documents, Washington, D.C. 20402, or your local Social Security Office:

Your Medicare Handbook

Your Social Security

Medicaid—Medicare: Which Is Which?

Introducing Supplemental Security Income

Information and referral services will be listed under several headings in the Yellow Pages, depending on their funding source, but should be able to lead you to legal aid or other public law groups that can give inexpensive legal advice on financial matters regarding the elderly.

The American Association of Retired Persons (AARP) has published several books on related matters. You can obtain a complete listing by writing them at 1909 K Street, N.W., Washington, DC 20049.

10
Talking about Health and Well-Being

Judy, in her late forties, was always very close with her mother, Alice, who was in her early seventies. They would visit at least once a week and talk on the telephone daily. Alice had expressed fears about ending up in a nursing home, and Judy had repeatedly promised that this would never happen.

At the same time, Judy was becoming concerned about small changes taking place in Alice's life. The apartment was not as clean as it used to be, and Alice couldn't hear the doorbell ring and was having trouble walking. Although Judy wanted to get her mother to the doctor, she felt that in so doing, she would be steering Alice toward a nursing home and thus breaking her promise.

Arthur, in his early eighties, had retired to Arizona with his wife, Thelma, who was in her seventies. Their two daughters, Irene and Cecilia, lived in Oregon, where the family had been raised. Irene, a nurse, had always been worried about Arthur's health, as he had had high blood pressure and did not take good care of his diet or his weight. Finally, after six months in Arizona, Arthur had a heart attack. After leaving the hospital, he decided that he and his wife should move back to where the children were.

After their return, Arthur would be found doing strenuous work around his new house and was eating salty foods and not attempting to lose any weight. Irene became increasingly distraught but felt that anything she said to him would make him angry and that he would deny that anything was wrong.

Randy was the middle-aged son of Alan, a man in his early eighties who was becoming more forgetful. Alan was also on medication that made him drowsy. Both of these conditions convinced Randy that his father should not be driving his car. Randy spent months agonizing how to tell his father not to drive. He tried hiding the car keys (his father then complained to Randy's wife, who returned them) and even moved his father's car to his house.

After the car was moved, Alan became angry and belligerent to Randy and Randy's wife, both of whom felt guilty for hiding the car. Finally, Randy decided that he had to discuss it. He sat his father down and told him he should not be driving. Alan argued with him, and later would raise the subject upon occasion or at times forget that the conversation had taken place. At the same time, he stopped making any serious efforts to get the car keys and drive the vehicle. (This was of only some comfort to Randy and his wife, who did not particularly enjoy the ensuing arguments.)

For Judy, talking with her parent about health and well-being meant honoring her promises while making sure that her mother got adequate medical care. For Irene and Cecilia, talking about health and well-being meant having to talk to Arthur about his reactions to his heart attack and confronting him about his current behavior. For Randy, talking to his father about health and well-being meant making a decision and living with the emotional consequences.

The issues related to health and well-being are varied. They encompass concerns about illness, disability, emotional problems, and what all these mean for the older person.

FACTS AND FIGURES

Bodily systems slow down somewhat with aging. However, a person's strength and vitality for tasks of day-to-day living should be adequate, with age-related changes showing up primarily when extra exertion is required. Most people are unaware of changes since they occur gradually over the span of many years. A sudden change suggests that there is an underlying condition that should be looked into immediately.

Eighty-six percent of the elderly have some sort of chronic condition, such as arthritis, diabetes, or a heart condition. Slightly more than half of these (46 percent) have some limitation of their activity because of their chronic conditions. At the same time, there are numerous examples of older persons living into their eighties and nineties in excellent health.

Concerns about health are linked to concerns about payment for health-care services. Most older Americans have Medicare, the governmental health insurance program for the elderly that began in 1965. Many subscribe to part B, a voluntary supplemental program in which the older person makes monthly payments in return for extended coverage for certain procedures and medical conditions. However, even with both parts of Medicare available, older persons spend more money out of their own pockets than they get from Medicare. They also spend a significantly larger proportion of their income than younger persons on health care.

Part of the reason older persons spend so much of their money on health care is that treatment of chronic conditions is not covered by Medicare, including routine office visits, eye care, foot care, hearing aids, or dental care, all of which are important and, if left unattended, can lead to serious disruptions in daily living. If your parent is faced with a medical visit to check out a complaint about walking, hearing, vision, or dentures, you are apt to find concern about payment existing along with the physical complaint.

It is beyond the scope of this text to review the symptoms of various diseases and conditions that affect the elderly. However, there are some signs that you should notice as indications of a change in health status.

- Sudden change in memory (See Chapter 12.)
- Noticeable change in gait (ability to walk)
- Complaints of pain (This one in particular is likely to be dismissed as a sign of "old age." Don't believe it—pain is due to specific causes, not merely to "age.")
- Changes in energy level or motivation
- Change in daily activity level and energy
- Changes in sleeping patterns (Many older people complain of difficulty in sleeping, which should not be overlooked, particularly if there is a noticeable change in sleeping patterns.)
- Signs of changes in perception, including decrease in home cleanliness, items being dropped, pots and pans not being used because they are "hard to handle," or difficulties hearing (which may be mistaken for "forgetting" when in fact things were not heard correctly)
- Falls, dizziness, or light-headedness
- Difficulties standing up from a chair or going up a flight of stairs

In the case of Judy and Alice at the beginning of this chapter, Alice had several soft signs of physical or emotional problems. Assuming that Judy could come up with an approach that included reassuring her mother that she would not go to a nursing home, Judy had good reason to be assertive in getting her mother to a physician to find the underlying causes of these changes, whether physical or mental or a combination of both.

While the most common mental health concerns of the elderly are depression and confusion, older persons are no less immune to "mental conditions" of all types than younger persons. Many older persons with mental health problems have had them for years and families have ignored them, confronted them, or even reinforced them.

Simply talking about mental health problems with your parents will not magically relieve their distress. The purposes of discussing mental health problems with your parents include showing concern, getting them to consider getting professional help (not an easy task in most cases), or attempting to break prior patterns that have made things worse. In so doing, most of the strategies mentioned in Chapter 6 still hold: be specific, take care of your needs, avoid defensive communication styles, be in touch with your own feelings (helplessness, frustration, etc.), discuss consequences of behavior rather than argue about its appropriateness, and practice what you are going to say before saying it.

If your parent has emotional difficulties, you are likely to feel frustrated, in pain, and guilty about somehow causing the problem, not doing enough to get help, or not being able to solve the problem. While understandable, none of these reactions is necessary, and they can make things worse if they come out in disguised ways.

Maureen, 72, had married Stewart, her second husband, five years earlier. Maureen had no children from her first marriage and had been pampered by her previous husband. Stewart had two daughters and one son. Stewart and Maureen lived in Arizona, where they had retired from a suburb of Detroit.

Stewart and Maureen had never gotten along particularly well, particularly because Maureen could not get the attention she was used to as Stewart became progressively ill. He had high blood pressure, diabetes, and a heart condition. At the same time, she had emphysema and asthma, and was complaining of feelings of worthlessness and lack of interest in any activities.

Stewart's daughters were concerned and visited Arizona several times a year. One, Angela, recognized that Maureen was depressed and thought she should either get therapy or take medication to control her symptoms. Maureen refused Angela's suggestion for a therapist and was reluctant to take the medication her physician recommended.

The second daughter, Rae, lived in Michigan and was involved with meditation and nutritional counseling. When she visited, she would get Stewart and Maureen to meditate, eat correctly, and take vitamins, all of which would stop the day she left.

Both daughters were frustrated at the failure of Stewart and Maureen to take care of themselves. Finally, on one visit, Rae "blew up" at them. (Actually, she spent time talking about how frustrated and hurt she felt over her parents' refusing to take care of themselves.) Although Maureen is still depressed and refusing professional help, Rae felt better after clearing the air. She stopped trying to make her parents do what they did not want to do in the first place, and instead began to talk with them, especially Maureen, about participating in interesting activities and events.

This case has several important points. First, the key signs of Maureen's condition were physical, which is not uncommon. Second, Maureen refused to seek professional help, which is also not uncommon. Third, it took a "clearing of the air" (which has elements of being assertive, using "I" statements and decreasing "telling" others what to do) for the daughter to feel better about herself and be able to begin to help her parents. Finally, although progress was made, its pace was set by the parents, not by the child's wishes.

Depression. Maureen's mental health problem was that most commonly associated with the elderly, depression. Contrary to popular belief, not all older persons are depressed, although estimates as to the number of older persons who have signs of depression go as high as 25 percent. There are some mental health professionals who believe that there is a form of depression specific to later life, but others disagree with them.

Depression is often divided into two types, reactive and endogenous. Reactive depression arises in response to recent events such as loss or illness. Endogenous depression is usually longer-lasting and is considered to be biochemical in nature and/or related to earlier learnings in the family. There are five signs of depression: feelings of sadness or boredom; lessened participation in normal activities; feelings of guilt or anxiety about one's abilities; physical symptoms such as stomachaches, loss of appetite, and headaches; and cognitive (thought) components, such as thinking that one is worthless or that "no one cares."

Talking about depression can be quite difficult, as many of the techniques and strategies for talking with your parents (such as reflection, active listening, and focusing on feelings) seem to deepen the depression and may result in *your* feeling overwhelmed and depressed. If you are fairly convinced that your parents are more depressed than is warranted by their situation, focus your discussions on getting them to seek help, reassure them that you do care for them (without becoming overwhelmed or trying heroically to lift their depression), and, at the same time, be sure that you do not become overwhelmed yourself as you try to play the part of a concerned child. Other possibilities that may help are ensuring that your parents have some form of exercise and opportunities to talk about how they are feeling. However, these alone are unlikely to take the place of competent mental health assistance, whether in the form of medication or a "talking" cure.

One last comment is necessary on this topic. Depression in the elderly has never been shown to be any less curable than depression in the young. So if your parent, a physician, another health professional, or even your own family members tell you nothing can be done, they are quite possibly wrong. The decision you will have to make (how hard to push for help when help is refused) will concern how much effort you want to put into this situation, as difficult as it is.

Suicide. Suicide among the elderly is more common than most people realize. Men over the age of 80 are among the highest at-risk groups. One of the saddest facts about suicide among the elderly is that there is an extremely high ratio of actual suicides to suicide attempts. What this means is that when older people talk about killing themselves, these statements should be taken seriously but calmly. If your parent starts to talk suicide or gives hints about it, find out if you can what is behind his or her concern, find out how well thought out his or her "plan" is, and "call in the marines" (again, gently). The "marines" can be a visiting nurse, social worker, physician, member of the clergy, or some other professional. By treating your parents' talk in this area as serious (rather than catastrophic or horrendous), you are both tending to their concerns and treating your parents as if you take them seriously, both of which are important in this type of case.

If you are faced with potential parental suicide, you are likely to be torn between a series of ethical, legal, medical, and personal dilemmas. You should feel free to consult with medical, legal, clergy, or mental health professionals for information and support for yourself as well as your parent.

Suspiciousness. The psychological explanation of inappropriate suspiciousness is that the older person is projecting his or her own fears onto others in the form of a delusional (incorrect) belief that they are out to spy, cheat, steal, or otherwise take advantage of him or her. Paradoxically, older persons who are suspicious also have great needs for intimacy and closeness, even though their behavior drives others away from them.

Family members frequently complain that older relatives are unnecessarily suspicious of others, including physicians, service agencies, or the federal bureaucracy, including Medicare and Social Security. Suspiciousness in and of itself does not mean that there is a clear-cut mental health problem, as it may be due to not understanding the situation or even due to physical losses, particularly hearing. It is not clear how prevalent serious mental health problems related to suspiciousness (paranoid reactions) are in the elderly, but even in minor forms, suspiciousness is one of the most frustrating issues for children of the elderly who are trying to help and protect them.

When confronted with suspiciousness, the following are recommended:

- Be honest.
- Be accepting of your parent without attacking (or accepting) the delusion (the belief that others are out to get them, spying on them, and so forth).
- Focus on consequences of their behavior rather than the truth or untruth of what they are saying.
- If the suspiciousness leads to disruptive actions (either with others or with family members), seek professional help *and* include your parent in the process from the beginning if at all possible.
- Finally, avoid taking responsibility for "causing" the belief. If you had nothing to do with the onset of suspiciousness, there is no need for guilt or other forms of self-blame.
- The case of Paul, Martin, and Martha in Chapter 5 is a classic example of how suspiciousness affects the family and how one son dealt with it. It took considerable time and patience to get Paul to a physician. There are other families who decide to put up with suspiciousness and live with it, which is certainly a viable choice as long as it does not cause them significant personal distress. The key points are that the family has to accept the person who is being suspicious, avoid guilt, and be honest and direct in their dealings with him or her.

Overconcern with Symptoms. Some older persons are overconcerned with physical symptoms. The technical term for a person who lives through an imaginary illness is *hypochondriasis*. From a practical view-point, it can be quite difficult to determine whether your parents' continual complaints about vague problems are a response to an illness, an emotional condition, or feeling unimportant and useless. Along with getting competent medical evaluation, you can also pay attention to what is going on in the rest of your parents' lives. Instead of talking about the way in which they may be symbolizing their emotional distress (which they will deny), focus your discussions on how they can get satisfaction out of contact with other people or new activities, or work with them to have pleasant and meaningful experiences that should, in turn, decrease their preoccupation with bodily functioning.

Medication

One of the facts of aging is that older persons use significantly more medication than younger persons. Medication includes prescribed drugs as well as over-the-counter remedies such as laxatives, aspirin, and cough syrup. Three-quarters of the elderly take some form of medication, and older persons use twice as much medication as younger people.

People with chronic conditions such as arthritis may have several medications in their possession dating back as far as ten years. It is not unknown for persons to "share pills," that is, to give each other a pill for similar conditions. One of the outcomes of using multiple medications and of careless self-medication can be a range of potentially dangerous side effects.

Overmedication and its impact on physical and mental health, according to some experts, is the leading reversible health problem of the elderly in this country. Medications have to be monitored carefully, as their improper use can lead to signs of depression and confusion as well as serious physical conditions.

Alcohol

Alcohol use, especially in conjunction with medication, is also a rising problem for the elderly. Changes in the body's ability to metabolize alcohol (as well as other drugs) means that its impact becomes greater with age. Estimates, although varied and somewhat uncertain, are that about 10 percent of the elderly have some problem with alcohol abuse. Families need to confront an older person who is potentially abusing alcohol and work hard to get him or her into appropriate treatment, either through organizations like Alcoholics Anonymous, treatment centers, or with physicians and other professionals who are increasingly responding to the needs of the older age group.

Nutrition

Research about the nutritional needs of the elderly shows that they need somewhat fewer calories than younger persons but that, in general, their needs for the basic food groups are similar. Many older persons show deficiencies in vitamins. Other nutritional problems include obesity, poor food preparation, and problems with chewing. Parenthetically, only one half of the elderly have any natural teeth, but few visit dentists, in part because Medicare does not pay for routine visits, and in part because of mistaken ideas that dentists can do little for older persons.

TALKING ABOUT SPECIFIC HEALTH ISSUES

Soft Signs of Illness

One of the most important purposes of talking about health with your parent is to help identify "soft" or subtle signs that indicate a change has taken place that warrants attention from health professionals. Some of the soft signs were mentioned earlier, including changes in perception, gait, activities, energy level, and memory, as well as dizziness, pain, and falls, to name a critical few.

The issues that arise in a discussion of symptoms are complex. For one thing, you or your parent may feel that any of the above symptoms are merely due to age, either out of belief or out of fear about what the real cause may be. Symptoms of disease can be different in older persons than in younger people, such as the type of discomfort felt in a heart attack, which for the elderly can feel remarkably like heartburn. Also, certain symptoms such as pain, loss of energy, or memory lapses may stem from a host of ailments, and it may require a significant effort to uncover the causes of the changes, an effort that you, your parent, or a physician may not want to make.

Since some of the costs of finding out what is the matter will be borne by your parent, it becomes a triple threat to pursue changes in functioning: first, there may be disbelief as to the significance of what you notice; second, there may be anxiety as to the possible causes of the change (which frequently may be bound up in the older person's fear of having an incurable illness, going to a nursing home, or otherwise having his or her life severely disrupted by the feared condition); and third, there can be concern about the cost of finding out what is wrong as well as the cost of ensuing treatment.

With these three factors in mind, talking about soft signs has to be approached sensitively but accurately. It is important to be specific about the issues you are raising with your parent. For example, you should talk about stumbling or dizzy spells rather than simply saying, "You've changed." It is also important to acknowledge, even if obliquely, the difficulty in going to the doctor when there is no obvious crisis. It may also be necessary to frame the concern as yours, and ask your parents to have something checked out to ease your worries about their well-being, reminding them that an ounce of prevention is worth a pound of cure. Above all, however, unless you are (literally or figuratively) going to drag them to the physician, the choice has to remain theirs.

Recovering from Surgery or Illness

Another important purpose of talking about health with your parents occurs when they are recovering from a hospitalization, a fall, a stroke, or some other condition. There are two aspects of these discussions: giving appropriate emotional support and talking about the rehabilitation process.

Appropriate Emotional Support. Illness carries with it fear, concerns about the future, and sometimes despair. The effects of these can be traumatic for the elderly. The older patient has lower reserves of strength and recuperative powers, as well as, at times, a diminished will to recover.

At times of illness, if I could wave a magic wand and have you remember anything, it might be the following: be reassuring without false reassurance; be empathic but not sympathetic; be connected but keep enough distance to prevent yourself from feeling overwhelmed. Your job is to listen with a hopeful attitude, knowing full well that your parent may not recover fully, that the road back is difficult, and that there is, indeed, suffering. This will not by any means be easy, but it can be one of the most beneficial things you do as a child or family member.

Rehabilitation. I am amazed at the extent to which medicine has improved the quality of life for older persons with certain conditions in the last two decades. For instance, surgery that would have been out of the question ten or twenty years ago, such as hip replacements, is common in persons in their seventies and eighties.

> Jessie, in her early eighties, had been plagued by circulation problems in one leg for ten years. Finally, after some urging by her family, she had a checkup and learned that the leg was in such bad shape that an amputation was necessary. Being of a tough and determined nature, she accepted the operation and learned to use an artificial leg.
>
> Her children, who had felt distraught about not "making" her go to a physician earlier, then insisted that she live with them. She adamantly refused, and returned to her two-story house (with bedroom and bathroom on the second floor). Despite her family's urging, she wanted to live by herself. After two years at home, she died.
>
> I spoke with John, one of her sons, after the funeral. "I wanted her to move in with us, but she refused," he said, "but at least she lived the way she wanted to."

John had been faced with several difficult decisions about talking with his mother before the operation, during recovery, and afterward. Although John's wishes were not realized, the fact that they were discussed and Jessie's desire to stay home was respected had to contribute to less guilt for John after she died.

In certain conditions, such as specific strokes, hip surgery, and cancer (depending on the site and how early the cancer is detected), substantial gains and even a fairly complete regaining of functional ability are possible. However, the fact is that one does not know for certain how much can be recovered. In addition, recovery can be quite tedious, with few obvious gains to show after weeks, even in cases where there is some certainty that improvement is possible.

You can play an important part by encouraging your parent's initial compliance with exercises, medication, or other aspects of recovery. You also need to be able to notice and reinforce small initial gains, along with having a realistic expectation of what is possible in terms of regaining functioning. By talking directly with your parents about how they are doing, by sharing frustrations as well as noticing (accurately) gains and potential, by acknowledging the difficulties and slowness of the process, you can provide a critical sense of reality and hope at a time when it is most needed.

Another important purpose of talking to your parent about health focuses on their adapting to changes that are, for all intents and purposes, not reversible. These changes may be due to chronic diseases, such as arthritis or diabetes. They may also be due to physical changes in vision, hearing, or mobility.

Using Aids. At times, chronic conditions are made easier by the use of an aid (also called an assistive device), such as glasses, a hearing aid, a walker, a wheelchair, or Velcro on clothing instead of hard-to-fasten buttons. There are many important issues for you to consider if you are in the position of talking to your parents about using these devices. One is any feeling your parents may have that they are now dependent or stigmatized by having an assistive device. They need to hear consistent and gentle reminders that assistive devices are designed to maintain *independence* and that "stigma" is a figment of others' imaginations, no matter how strongly the stigma is felt.

Another issue is that with a new device, whether it is a hearing aid or a walker, there needs to be hope tempered with reasonable expectations for ease of use, comfort, and how much the assistive device will really help. You will have to maintain a delicate balance in your encouragement of use between hope and the realities of rehabilitation.

Perhaps the biggest problem people face in using assistive devices arises in going out in public. Not only will they be self-conscious about using the device but they may have to cope with looks, comments, and inappropriate offers of help from a public that is uncomfortable about wheelchairs, blindness, or any disability. You can be of tremendous assistance to your parents by discussing these issues in advance and actually becoming their coach, practicing with them how they will handle those assaults on their self-esteem when they arise so that they use the devices to help themselves in public.

An important part of your discussions in this area will be how you handle your own reactions to the fact that your parents now use an artificial support to walk, hear, or see. Hiding feelings of embarrassment (or acting as if they do not occur) is not recommended. Rather, you need to address them directly—by yourself, with a friend, or with a professional. You may choose to share them with your parents, not as feelings that preclude their using the aid, but rather as naturally occurring reactions that need to be overcome so that you both can get on with the business of living and adapting.

Acceptance of Changes

Acceptance of a change is one goal for handling limitations. Acceptance does not mean giving up, nor does it mean denying anger or frustration. Rather, acceptance means living with a full realization of the realities of a condition without giving up on one's ability to live, grow, and work on the challenges and problems created by the condition. Acceptance does not have to be passive, but it does imply that there is more to living with a condition than being depressed about it. One of your purposes in discussing health changes with your parents is to help them (as well as yourself) learn to live fully with the realities of the changes, to actively accept the changes, cope with necessary adaptations, and not make the conditions the focal point of your lives.

In the case of Arthur presented at the beginning of this chapter, his overexertion and poor eating habits after his heart attack probably stemmed from a refusal to accept limitations. In a case like this, the family needs to talk with him and listen to his fears, be supportive and accepting, but also work hard on encouraging him to make changes as a way of living as opposed to a giving up on life. In other cases, such as that of Jessie, the family needs to allow parents to live their own lives and acknowledge underlying feelings of guilt and fear as *their* reactions.

Medications

As I mentioned earlier, the misuse of medications by the aged is a major health concern. Families can assist older persons by talking with them about their medications. At the same time, being questioned about the use of medicines may seem an invasion of privacy to some older persons. For others, it will be a relief to have someone review with them:

• When medications should be taken
• Under what conditions (e.g., with meals or on an empty stomach)
• How often
• How to know the medication is working
• How to know when the medication is not working

One question that may come up is whether or not your parents are actually taking the pills when they are supposed to. Other topics include taking medicine that is out of date, using several physicians for different conditions who prescribe medications that interact dangerously, or refusing to take medication that makes your parent feel worse than the symptoms it was prescribed for (such as certain drugs for high blood pressure).

For each of these topics, you have to be sure of your facts about the condition, the appropriateness of the medication, and the signs that make you concerned. You also have to be prepared to hear reasons for noncompliance such as "The medicine is not working," "It costs too much," "I was feeling better so I didn't take it," and a host of other half truths (and perhaps some whole truths).

After being a good detective to rule out certain complaints (e.g., "It doesn't work"), you may need to pursue the point assertively with your parent, keeping in mind that the following underlying reasons may explain why he or she is not using the medicine correctly:

- Taking medication for the rest of one's life (as is the case for certain conditions, such as high blood pressure) seems to demonstrate a loss of independence and a state of continually being sick.
- In a related way, taking a pill is a constant reminder that the person taking it is ill, a patient, and dependent.
- Many older persons do not like spending so much money on medications.
- It can be difficult for older persons to find any obvious changes in their bodies as positive results that the medication is working.

Preventive Measures

Preventive measures include anything you would want your parent to do to ward off illness, disability, or other physical harm. Topics included under this heading include exercise, nutrition and dietary habits, stopping smoking, and avoiding exposure to potential physical harm.

A range of ethical and practical concerns emerge under this heading. For example, do older persons have the right to stay alone when they are in danger of falling? Should an elderly woman with a heart condition be "allowed" to eat salty foods? Does a diabetic get a piece of birthday cake—even a small one—on his ninetieth birthday?

I do not have hard-and-fast answers to these questions, but would urge you to carefully consider the implications of what you say and how you say it. If you are anxious, blaming, placating, or otherwise incongruent in the way you discuss these matters, you will fail to make much of a difference. Admittedly, you may have no success with assertion and being straight either, but your points are more likely to be taken to heart, and you can take some comfort in that you have approached the issues in the way most likely to succeed.

Also, remember that food and exercise, to name two of the preventive areas, are interrelated with history, role, and day-to-day living. Having to give up ethnic favorites or undergo some physical discomfort for a greater benefit in the future initially represents to your parents the loss of a form of pleasure and identity. For that reason, it will not always be easy to make changes.

Driving

Driving an automobile is considered a right by most of the populace. Many Americans are lost without their cars, which represent individuality, "freedom of the road," and, for the elderly, an important and sometimes the sole means of transportation to shopping, services, and health care. Men are especially prone to consider their use of the automobile an important right and part of their identity.

Some of the concerns that arise about an older person's driving are reaction speed, manual dexterity, vision (especially at night, when age-related changes decrease visual acuity), a mental or physical condition that limits the ability to know where one is, and the use of medications that could cause the driver to fall asleep. These conditions can result in difficulties in night driving, in negotiating entry to and exit from highways, and in handling congested areas.

The truth is that generally older persons are safer drivers than younger persons. However, many of us know older persons who seem to be potentially unsafe drivers. And, of course, unsafe drivers are a potential danger to others as well as to themselves.

Judging by the experience of some people who have had to tell their parents they should not drive, like Randy in the beginning of this chapter, it seems that many persons who appear to be unsafe drivers deny that they are not in full control of their reactions and abilities. Families have been known to try a range of strategies to get the potentially dangerous older driver off the road, including offering to have their parent take driving lessons to let an impartial observer evaluate his or her driving. One friend has suggested that one might drive behind an older relative for a few miles to get a good idea of how well he or she is are doing.

Some families have discussed how the parent can avoid dangerous situations, as by agreeing not to drive at night or by finding alternative routes to avoid difficult highway access points or congested areas. Or family members may persuade the elderly to stop driving by talking about the costs of keeping up a car compared with using public transportation or taxis as a substitute. Some have even worked diligently to familiarize their parents with the public transportation system to aid them make the transition to being without a car.

The important strategies and skills to remember are that you should be direct, assertive, empathic (as this is a serious loss to contemplate), and logical without escalating. If your parent's continuing to drive is a serious question, you also have to be prepared to take certain steps (including insisting on a physical or eye examination) if things do not go well.

Ideally, your parent should participate in the decision, even if it means finding points that you can both agree on that do not result in a loss of face (such as agreeing that other motorists are too dangerous or the costs of keeping a car are too great). However, if, like Randy at the beginning of this chapter, you choose to hide keys, spark plug wires, or a license, realize that you are acting in ways that sacrifice honesty and trust in your relationship. You may have to live with parental anger at the loss of independence that is directed at you and be willing to pay this price for eliminating a potentially serious danger. My personal preference is for there to be some sort of negotiated agreement with discussion rather than a power play, in part because the power play gives your parent a strong message that he or she cannot handle matters and that they are being taken out of his or her hands.

Getting Help at Home

Another difficult area related to health and functioning is the issue of hiring workers to help with chores, activities of daily living (e.g., bathing and dressing), or housekeeping. It is not uncommon for older persons, especially women for whom being a homemaker was an important source of identity, to not want to have help in the home. There can be denial (like the older woman who claims that the dirt noticed in her kitchen is just from that day), refusal, and complaints that the help will cost too much or that helpers will not do things correctly. There may be complaints that the help will be the "wrong kind of people" (age does not seem to soften racial or ethnic prejudices) or anger that covers the fear of loss of identity and independence that having help in the home represents.

In contrast to the issue of driving, which involves clear harm to the driver and others, there is less of a clear potential harm if help in the home is refused. Your parent does have the right to refuse and may well do it even in the face of rational arguments about the need for properly prepared meals, a clean residence, or help with some chores and errands.

If you have to talk about the need for help, it will be important to do research to find the types of help that can be obtained, the cost, and the specific tasks that certain types of workers will and will not do. Carefully assess your parents' needs and make sure everyone, including your parents, understands the limits of the paid help's work and that you can discuss any concerns or questions that arise after help begins to come into the home.

The following guides may be helpful in talking about help coming into the home:

- Use specifics rather than generals. Do not waste your time talking about how your parents are not taking care of themselves. It will be more fruitful to focus on the specific tasks that need to be done by another person.
- Be aware of any guilt that may make you inadvertently imply either that the help is taking your place or that you can cover when the help is not available.
- Focus on consequences rather than beliefs. For example, remind your parent of the negative consequences of not having this particular form of assistance available.
- Be assertive and direct, without hostility, and with repetition of key points (e.g., "Mom, you may not like it, it may not be perfect, but if I said it once, I'll say it a hundred times to you: you need to have help

in to clean. If you continue the way you are doing, you will end up in either a hospital or a nursing home").

- Call in the "marines": get the family physician, lawyer, clergy, or some other authority figure to "bless" your parent's having help with the understanding that the minimum amount of help is being given so as to ensure the maximum amount of independence.
- Be an active listener. You can acknowledge the sense of loss, violation of privacy, or whatever your parents are feeling and then remind your parents that, even with these feelings, which are real, strong, and important, it still stands that help is needed for them to remain at their highest level of functioning.

Consumer Issues

There is one last purpose that you may have in talking with your parent about health: being a wise consumer of health services. This may mean getting second opinions about medical matters, changing physicians if there is concern about the quality of care your parent is getting, noting the effects of medications on your parent, figuring out how to reduce the costs of health care (e.g., using generic instead of brand-name drugs), and protecting the rights of your parent in health settings.

Talking about some consumer issues will not be easy. Imagine the difficulty in getting your mother to change physicians after spending six months just to persuade her to go see one! Similarly, it can be difficult when the physician you want to change has been treating your parent for years.

Many of the concerns is this chapter relate to using professional services. Much of your talking with your parents will focus on when and how to go for help and how to handle reactions to what can (and cannot) be done for a given condition. I advise you to become educated consumers, as the health-care system, payments, and care of the elderly will become more complex in the future. The references listed here can be of help to you in this task.

RESOURCES

Breuer, J. *Handbook of Assistive Devices for the Handicapped Aged.* New York: Haworth Press, 1982.

Edinberg, M. *Mental Health Practice with the Elderly.* Englewood Cliffs, N.J.: Prentice-Hall, 1985. A college text written for professionals working with the elderly and their families. It reviews major mental problems of the aged and their treatment.

Graedon, J. *The People's Pharmacy: Two.* New York, Avon, 1980. One of several guides to medications for the lay person.

Hale, G. (ed.). *The Source Book for the Disabled.* New York: Bantam Books, 1981. An excellent inexpensive how-to book on all aspects of living for the disabled person.

Hooyman, N. R., and W. Lustbader. *Taking Care: Supporting Older People and Their Families.* New York: Free Press, 1986. An excellent book about dealing with the multiple problems facing older persons and their families. It gives practical solutions to many of the complicated problems discussed in these chapters.

Horne, J. *Caregiving: Helping an Aging Loved One.* Washington, D.C.: American Association of Retired Persons, Scott Foresman Co., 1985. Designed to give people basic information about a range of health and mental health issues and focuses on responsibilities and strategies for the caregiver.

Norback, J. (ed.). *Sourcebook of Aid for the Mentally and Physically Handicapped.* New York: Van Nostrand Reinhold, 1984.

Porcino, J. *Growing Older, Getting Better: A Handbook for Women in the Second Half of Life.* Reading, Mass.: Addison-Wesley, 1983. Section II focuses on biological changes and illnesses of older women.

Silverstone, B., and H. K. Hyman. *You and Your Aging Parent.* Mount Vernon, N.Y.: Consumers Union, 1982. One of the first and best guides on coping with aging parents. It covers some of the issues in this book, but also has more emphasis on how to locate and obtain services.

Simonson, W. *Medications and the Elderly: A Guide for Promoting Proper Use.* Rockville, Md.: Aspen Books, 1983.

11
Talking about Confusion

Larry, a man in his early eighties, had been diagnosed as having Alzheimer's disease. After he had been maintained in his own home for about a year, his family had him institutionalized because he was incontinent and could not be left alone. Like many Alzheimer's patients, Larry did not exhibit much feeling and said little unless spoken to.

A few months after his move into the nursing home, his daughter, Wendy, came to visit as she did every week. "How's it going?" she asked.

"I'm losing my mind," Larry said, sounding depressed.

Wendy did not know what to say to him, as he had never been told directly what his diagnosis was and he would probably forget anyway if she told him.

At a major hospital, an unusual program existed for several years. The program was a family-oriented assessment project for elderly persons with confusion. I sat in on one discussion with an older person who in all likelihood had Alzheimer's disease, along with his wife, daughter, and son-in-law. Michael sat quietly throughout the discussion of the tests and results. Finally, the physician in charge of the conference told all of them that Michael might have a dementia, an irreversible condition. There was an understandable silence in the room.

Finally Michael spoke. "I am happy," he said. "I am in no pain, I have the love of my family, I am lucky to have been alive this long."

The families of both Larry and Michael had to grapple with what to say to their parent about confusion as well as the painful issue of caring for a parent with limited abilities. It was unfortunate that Wendy did not have the appropriate resources available to help her and her father cope with his depression, whereas Michael and his family ended up in a setting that encouraged them to talk together about what was going on.

Confusion is one of the least understood issues related to aging. For years, terms such as *senility*, *confusion*, and *old* have been thought to mean the same things by many older persons, their families, physicians, and other professionals who work with the elderly.

Perhaps because of the fears related to being confused and helpless or having Alzheimer's disease, older persons and their children are reluctant to discuss the small signs that *could* represent a serious condition. The reluctance is understandable as an attempt to carry on with one's life (the positive side of denial), but can also mean that potentially reversible conditions end up causing serious and unnecessary damage to older persons and their families because they were not given adequate attention early on.

Even if the reason for some changes in memory, orientation, or judgment is a condition that cannot be arrested, there is still ample reason to talk with your parent who has the condition. People with serious illnesses may be frightened or puzzled by their lack of memory. Some may try to cover it up. Others may be easily agitated, either for physiological reasons or as an emotional reaction to the changes that are taking place in their bodies. If others around the person stop talking with him or her, if they withdraw emotionally, this will be noticed and felt. The reaction of the older person may then be withdrawal, hesitancy in trying to communicate, and depression.

An additional reason for talking with the confused person is that, for some cases, there is the possibility that some cognitive abilities can improve or at least be maintained by actively "working the gray matter." It may be important to remind people who they are, where they are, the day of the week, the names of colors, or other tasks that seem simple to the rest of us. Whatever the content, the communication should be done congruently and in a positive manner, without condescension or exasperation.

This last point cannot be stressed enough. It is sad to witness the way people deal with a confused elderly parent when their own pain comes out in indirect ways, often in baby talk, the assumption that their parent cannot understand them, or the patronizing manner in which they talk with their parent. Part of the pain comes from knowing that the confused person is no longer the person she or he was one, two, or ten years ago. Part may also come from guilt over not doing enough early on in the illness. Part may also come from anger resulting from frustration over having your parent forget simple matters, such as your name, and then ask you over and over who you are. Part may come from spending enormous amounts of energy, time, and money to care for a parent who slowly loses cognitive functioning as well as control over bodily functioning. Finally, part of the difficulty in talking with a confused parent may come from simply not knowing what to say to someone who gives few obvious cues that he or she understands what is being said.

> Henry, in his late thirties, was talking about his father, Louis, 72. Louis had Alzheimer's disease and had been institutionalized. It had been hard for Henry and his mother, Jeanne, as both had spent several years caring for Louis at home.
> "When we go see him, we never know if he can understand us or make sense out of what we say," Henry said. "But you have to believe that once in a while, when his eyes change just a bit, when he looks like he might have some idea of who we are, he knows for just that moment. He can't tell us, of course, but we always talk to him as if he could understand us."

Henry's message is simple but often forgotten: there has to be a spirit of hope tempered with a sense of reality. Your connections with an Alzheimer's patient who is severely disabled may be infrequent and brief. You may not know for certain that he knows who he is and who you are. At the same time, the looks, the occasional smiles and pieces of communication between two humans, will be the important parts of your time together.

FACTS AND DEFINITIONS

Confusion refers to fairly specific problems that some older persons (and, occasionally, younger persons) have that indicate that their brains are not functioning properly. Specifically, there may be difficulties in *judgment* (ability to make decisions), *affect* (emotions), *memory* (remembering events, directions), *cognition* (ability to think, do simple computations, understand abstractions), and *orientation* (knowing *person* [who one is], *place* [one's address or the place where one is at the moment], and *time* [day, date, and season]).

Alertness refers to the energy level and ability of the individual to hear what is said, communicate, and otherwise function in the realm of perception. It is possible to be alert and confused, confused but not alert, or not alert but not confused (the last condition is one most frequently seen in college students during lectures). Thus Alzheimer's patients may be able to carry on an intelligent conversation, the only hint that anything is wrong being that afterward they have no idea whom they were talking with or what they said.

Delirium refers to a range of conditions that may lead to confusion. Many of these conditions are reversible, with confusion being one by-product of another problem. Delirium is often characterized by rapid onset, short duration, fluctuations in abilities, changes in alertness (including a sense of "clouding" or difficulties in perceptual processes), disturbed sleep cycle, and hallucinations (seeing or hearing things that are not there).

Dementia is the technical term for diseases that cause brain-cell death and, at present, irreversible losses of memory, judgment, personality, and bodily functioning. There are two types of dementia, the best known being senile dementia of the Alzheimer's type (Alzheimer's disease).

Approximately 15 percent of the elderly have some form of confusion; the percentage doubles for persons over 85. Slightly more than half of the persons with confusion (or 7 percent of the elderly) have delirium, and 8 percent have a form of dementia, most frequently Alzheimer's disease.

Alzheimer's disease has received a significant amount of attention in the media. It is a slow, debilitating condition characterized initially by small changes in functioning and leading eventually, in many cases, to losses in all the areas mentioned above, as well as incontinence, difficulties with judgment, and behavioral problems such as wandering. Although it is not always the case, it is common to find Alzheimer's patients who seem out of touch with others and almost vegetative near the end of life.

There is no magical or consistent way of predicting how long a person will live with the condition, how he or she will progress, or even whether the losses described above will definitely occur in a given case. Some research suggests that life span is about five years after diagnosis. However, when those diagnosed are already in their eighties, this does not represent a substantial shortening of the life span.

Research has showed that there is, in all likelihood, a biological basis for Alzheimer's disease (probably a slow-acting virus) and that genetics may well contribute to its onset. This does *not* mean that if one or even both of your parents have the condition, you will inevitably come down with it yourself. At the same time, family members do frequently fear that they will come down with Alzheimer's disease if a relative has it.

Many, at some level, mistakenly think that it can be "caught" by being near the patient.

Several factors make the care of the Alzheimer's patient a "thirty-six-hour day" (the title of an excellent resource text on the topic). Persons with Alzheimer's disease can have frustrating memory losses, can wander and get lost, can perform unsafe acts (such as leaving a stove on and forgetting they did so), can be incontinent without being aware that urinary or fecal matter has been passed, or can act in other ways that are upsetting to the family, including crying, repeating phrases, or, if speech is affected, moaning or uttering unintelligible sounds.

Families who care for Alzheimer's patients find themselves with a range of reactions that include anger, frustration, guilt, despair, exhaustion, and depression. Some research suggests that over half of persons caring for an Alzheimer's patient become depressed and can benefit from professional therapy or counseling.

Programs that offer assistance to such families have grown, including "respite" care services, which allow families time off from the day-to-day caretaking, and support groups, which hold meetings that get people with similar problems together to talk about coping with the illness and sharing information about help. One national group, the Alzheimer's Disease and Related Disorders Association (ADRDA), has local chapters throughout the country. Its address is listed at the end of this chapter.

PURPOSES IN TALKING ABOUT CONFUSION

Given all the possibilities and nuances of care for the confused person, there are several important reasons to talk with the person who has Alzheimer's disease.

Getting Information

One important reason is simply to find out the degree to which your parent is confused. You can ask questions about what he or she knows and does not know (attempting to be neutral no matter what the reply and then reporting your findings to a physician or other health professional). You may also ask your parent (*gently*) if he or she is aware of or concerned about any lapses you noticed, again remembering to be neutral and to focus on specifics, not generals, and not to argue if you are given a defensive explanation of why something was forgotten. If you are getting information, remember that your purpose is exactly that, to be a reporter so that others can assess what is really going on with your parent.

Even if the underlying reason is something as difficult to handle as Alzheimer's disease (which, however, cannot be diagnosed definitively in many cases), both you and your parent will do better in the long run with an accurate understanding of the condition than if you act as though nothing were the matter or otherwise deny reality. You may have to deal with sadness, grief, and other distressing emotions if you find out the underlying cause of apparent confusion, but handling these emotions directly can result in much better feelings about yourself (and about your parent) than avoiding them.

Giving Information

I am saddened at how often families do not give an elderly member accurate information about his or her condition. Persons who are confused can be scared, fearful, depressed, and worried about themselves, and yet, for what I believe are primarily defensive reasons, the family will collude with a physician and avoid telling the person that he or she has a disease that affects thinking, that the disease has a name, or that the condition is serious.

I am not recommending that you automatically tell your parent that he or she has Alzheimer's disease (whatever that may mean to your parent, which will also influence how you break the news), but rather that you carefully consider giving information that accurately describes the condition along with assurance that you are not abandoning your parent, that you love him, and that even though there are losses, you will stand by him to pay attention to what he *can* do and feel rather than dwelling only on what he can no longer do, think, or say. Many will deny that anything is wrong, at which point you would do well not to argue, as that will only escalate the denial.

Telling people about their medical condition is not easy. Yet not telling them can result in more fear than is warranted. (How often, I wonder, do Alzheimer's patients who are not told about their condition think, "My God, this must be *so* bad that they cannot even discuss it"?) It will be made even more difficult if the person who is told forgets and continues to ask what is wrong, making it tempting to say, "Nothing is wrong" or "You won't understand anyway," yelling, getting upset, or withdrawing. Glossing over the question or having those other reactions will only inhibit your parents from taking the risk to interact with you (which, after all, is an important part of what you are likely to want from them) and also deprives them of the right to know what is going on in their bodies.

Other aspects of giving information include telling your parent that a change in routine is taking place (changes are difficult for many persons with confusion), that legal matters are being changed, or that your parent has to go into an institution. Too often, I believe, families avoid these discussions, which can only contribute to long-term guilt and discomfort for the parent.

Helping the Confused Person to Maintain Contact with Reality

One of the most useful purposes of talking with your parents can be to help them maintain contact with you and others in their environment. One of the sets of techniques for doing so, *reality orientation*, has been developed to help older persons maintain their sense of orientation to person, place, and time. It entails rewarding the person by saying "Good," "Right," or some other form of encouragement when he or she correctly identifies the day, date, or your name. Another technique, *sensory awareness*, entails presenting simple choices or questions concerning sensory perception (including identifying a color, sound, taste, or smell) and rewarding a correct response by the confused person.

There has been some criticism of techniques like these, particularly when they are done in a mechanical, uncaring manner or when the older person is asked questions that are either too difficult or simple for his or her mental abilities. At the same time, many families have found it useful to have a set of simple skills that allow them to have contact with their parents in ways that are rewarding to both of them. Using techniques like reality orientation and sensory awareness can offer one set of guidelines for helping the older person maintain contact with others in the environment.

Additionally, you can spend useful time with parents who are confused by talking about what they *can* remember, particularly incidents from the past. The idea of using *reminiscence* in this manner makes sense in that many older persons like to reminisce, you both can learn new things about your family, and that reminiscence can bring back pleasant memories and feelings that have been forgotten because of present circumstances. (However, if the past is really unpleasant or your parent has a tendency to remember only the negative and painful aspects of the past, you may want to keep reminiscence to a minimum or focused on more positive aspects.)

Sharing Feelings

You and your parents may both need to talk about feelings—your feelings about caring for them and theirs about their condition, their lives, or even their guilt at being dependent on you. While you do not *have* to share every frustration as it occurs, some "getting straight" time may be beneficial to you both.

> Pauline, the daughter of Evelyn, an Alzheimer's patient, had been going to support group meetings for several months, bringing her mother with her. They lived in a small community outside of Cincinnati where it was hard to find someone to stay with Evelyn for these evening meetings. So Evelyn accompanied Pauline but generally stayed in another room with other patients who had been brought by their sons and daughters.
> Upon occasion, Evelyn would wander into the group meeting, at which point Pauline would stop talking about her problems with her mother. The group leader asked me what to do about keeping Evelyn out of the meetings so that Pauline could speak more freely. I suggested that while having time away to vent feelings had its place, Pauline needed time to talk with Evelyn so that sharing her frustration would not come as a surprise or be taken by Evelyn as a "blaming" statement about herself.

Helping One Parent Cope with the Other's Confusion

People often have mixed and varied feelings about their involvement in the care of a parent who is confused when the other parent is the primary caregiver. Not only do you have to worry about the condition underlying one parent's confusion, but you have to deal with a changing marital relationship and the dynamics of the three of you (Mom, Dad, and you).

While your healthy parent may have primary responsibility for the care of the other, you can play an important role by being a sounding board, a "window" to reality, and an information seeker. You may find yourself confronting your parent with the need to seek help for the other parent, to accept help with caring for the other, or even to make the difficult decision to institutionalize a husband or wife.

There will be times when any input you attempt will not be well received, times when your input will be viewed as "meddling," or even times when your input will mean that you somehow get involved in doing more than you wish to or can handle. You will have to weigh possible outcomes with your own emotional pulls to be a "good child" and a good husband/wife/mother/father/worker and with your need to decide how and how much you will help one parent deal with the other's confusion.

Planning

It is of the utmost importance that the older confused person be included in planning major and minor changes in routine. Changes will be hard for the person with dementia or delirium to handle, and planning will *not* eliminate difficulties. However, a sense of inclusion is comforting, although you may have to explain the changes when they happen if your parent does not remember being in on the planning.

RESPONSES OF THE ELDERLY

Several reactions older persons commonly have to confusion include denial, apathy, "emotional lability" (being easy to anger), and covering up the existence of any problem. If you think you are getting one of these, please remember that while the reaction may be directed against you, it in no way is meant as a statement about you.

There is also the possibility that you are concerned about confusion when, in fact, there is none and the response of your parents is bewilderment, fear (that something could be wrong), suspicion (about what you might be trying to "pull"), or even anger that you think they are less capable than they are. (Of course, it is also possible that you will get appreciation for your taking the effort to find information or help.) These negative responses are understandable and human but may not be comfortable to receive. My advice on how to weather these storms is to be assertive and positive. That is, state that you are concerned and that you care enough to want to be sure that your parents have no signs of problems, but if they did have signs, you would want everything to be done to keep them in the best physical and mental health possible.

INFORMATION NEEDED

Depending on your purpose, you may need some important information before talking with your parent about confusion. First and foremost, if your discussion gets into diagnosis or a specific condition, you should have some idea about what the condition is, what it means to your parent, and what you all can expect as time goes by.

If your discussion involves planning, you may need to gather information about types of help available, how easy it is to obtain such help, and costs (including coverage by insurance, entitlements, or other programs). The information-finding process can be frustrating and confusing, even to someone who works in the helping professions.

STEPS AND STRATEGIES

The following guidelines should be helpful in talking with confused older parents.

- Be calm.
- Talk to your parents as though you expect them to be able to understand you.
- Be concrete rather than abstract.
- Give facts in answer to questions or incorrect statements.
- Ask your parents to relax and speak slowly, and encourage them to take their time.
- Give clear explanations, give examples, and be prepared to repeat them without showing impatience.
- Use all sensory channels; use touch to maintain contact.
- Make your questions simple.
- Make your answers to your parents' questions clear.
- Do not agree to things you do not understand.
- Do not pretend to understand rambling or confusing statements.
- Avoid patronizing or using "baby talk."
- Avoid unnecessary confrontation about confusion. Thus, you might say, "I do not understand that; please say it again," instead of saying, "You are confused; say it again."

- Use props (e.g., a message board, calendars, clocks, pictures) to help you and your parent if you are engaged in "reality orientation." Also, try to make sure that there are cues in the environment to help your parent remember things without having to ask others.
- If you are giving instructions, break them down into small steps and have them written down so your parents can refer to them as they need to.

OUTCOMES

Unlike some of the other topics in this book, one of the most important things you have to do to manage successfully with a confused parent is to carefully redefine your appreciation of outcomes. What for you may be commonplace, such as remembering your name, may be quite difficult for someone who is confused. Similarly, for your parent to try to think about an event or a place and to remember it can be an achievement requiring intense effort.

While you will undoubtedly feel the pain of the losses of parents who suffer from dementia, you can gain a sense of hope and compassion by paying attention to what they *can* do, any efforts at personal contact, and other signs of the flame of human existence, no matter how faint its light. Developing realistic expectations of the outcomes of talking with your confused parent can be difficult. It requires grieving and learning new ways of communicating on your part, but it will help you avoid unnecessary depression and bad feelings for the duration of the condition.

> Claire was a woman in her eighties who had Alzheimer's disease. Her daughter, Geraldine, had been working with a family counselor who asked that Claire attend a session. Claire sat silently through the session, nodding her head, occasionally answering questions directed to her, but not seeming to understand the issues being discussed.
>
> As they stood up to leave at the end, Claire turned to her daughter and said, quite clearly, "I am sorry for the pain I have caused you in the past. I wish I could do it over again."

This story shows how important parts of an elderly parent's personality may still be intact despite the confused state. They can best be reached by hopefulness for contact, attentiveness, and the expectation that your love and concern are being received, even if no obvious return is being made.

WHAT YOU WANT TO SAY, WHAT YOU CAN LIVE WITH SAYING

In one sense, what you want to say to parents who are confused is no different from what you want to say to those who are not. That is, there are concerns about the past, about the present, about them, and about other family members that you might wish to discuss. And you should consider doing so, even if there is a chance that what you say will be forgotten. In so doing, you will be making the best peace possible for both you and your parent.

The part about what you have to say can be quite painful. You might have to say you cannot take care of your parent, that your parent has to go into a nursing home, or other equally difficult things. You can also avoid saying these things at all, but the consequences of doing so, in the long run, are much worse for all of you than saying what is true for you, as is shown in the following story.

Harriet was one of three children who took turns taking care of their mother, Colleen, who had become increasingly confused over several years. Colleen would spend four months a year living in each child's household. The family was close and had practically sworn never to put their mother in a nursing home.

However, after several years, Colleen got worse. She began to wander, would leave the stove on, could not remember who any of her children or in-laws were, and could not be by herself for any period of time. She fell several times and finally ended up in the hospital with broken ribs.

Harriet, at whose house Colleen had been staying, decided with her sisters to have her mother put into a nursing home. Colleen was initially told she was only going there to recover from her rib injury and continually asked Harriet when she was going home.

Finally, after six weeks of feeling guilty, Harriet decided to tell her mother. "Mom," she said, "you really can't take care of yourself anymore, and we can't take care of you at our house. You are going to live here now permanently."

Colleen listened and nodded agreement. For the next few weeks, she would forget what she had been told, and Harriet would gently remind her. From what Harriet reported to me later on, her mother did not seem particularly upset over the news, and possibly was a bit relieved to know why she was staying in "that place" for so long. Harriet also mentioned that she felt much better having discussed matters with her mother.

Here, once again, much of the difficulty in talking with the parent rested with the child. The reasons for not talking with Harriet, such as "She wouldn't understand" or "She would forget," were really masking the pain, guilt, and sense of failure Harriet felt when, in reality, she and the rest of her family had been heroic and were making the best decision for Colleen and themselves.

Handling the issues related to an parent's confusion and underlying conditions is only partially addressed by talking about it. The resources listed below can give you more information as well as ways to get in touch with experts and other children of the elderly with similar problems.

RESOURCES

Cohen, D., and C. Eisdorfer. *The Loss of Self: A Family Resource for the Care of Alzheimer's Disease and Related Disorders*. New York: W. W. Norton, 1986. Perhaps the best book on the topic along with *The 36-Hour Day*. The authors offer comprehensive guides for families on obtaining appropriate medical and social care, plus devote significant thought to how families can cope with the older confused person.

Help Begins at Home, International Center for the Disabled, 340 East Twenty-fourth Street, New York, NY 10010. This pamphlet is an excellent guide to basic care and communication issues with the confused older person.

Mace, N. L., and P. V. Rabins. *The 36-Hour Day*. New York: Warner Books, 1981. An excellent book on the topic, it also includes many practical hints on handling behavior associated with Alzheimer's disease.

Powell, L., and K. Courtice. *Alzheimer's Disease: A Guide for Families*. Reading, Mass.: Addison-Wesley, 1983.

Zarit, S. H.; N. K. Orr; and J. M. Zarit. *The Hidden Victims of Alzheimer's Disease: Families under Stress*. New York: New York University Press, 1985.

The Alzheimer's Disease and Related Disorders Association, 70 East Lake Street, Suite 600, Chicago, IL 60601, (312) 853-3060, is a nonprofit organization with chapters throughout the United States. It is the major organization devoted to the disease and family support.

12
Talking about Death and Dying

Adeline, 89, had cancer of the pancreas, a condition that is usually fatal. Her daughter, Pat, who had loved and cared for her mother for over ten years since her father died, was told of the diagnosis by the doctor. After discussing things with her two sisters, Pat decided that Adeline should not know about her diagnosis because "It would kill her." At the same time, Adeline talked to nurses, aides, and clergy about being afraid that she was going to die and asked why no one would talk to her about her condition.

At a senior center, I was giving a talk entitled "You and Your Middle-Aged Children." It was well attended by older persons concerned about how to relate to their middle-aged offspring. At one point, I asked them, "What topics do your children have the most difficulty with when you want to discuss them?" The overwhelming first response was death, followed closely by finances and sex.

Both of these stories reflect the difficulties family members can have in talking about death with each other. At the same time, death is an integral part of human experience. It is feared, questioned, denied, coped with, and studied. Until the late 1960s, it was a topic that was not commonly discussed by physicians, nurses, social workers, psychologists, and others in the helping professions with their clients or with each other. Since that time there has been at least some demystification of the process of dying and an interest in how we can help others as they approach the end of their lives.

While talking about death is not easy, there are potential benefits for all family members from talking about feelings, perceptions, beliefs, fears, and concerns about death. In addition, there are times when talking about death is important for psychological, personal, and ethical reasons.

FACTS AND FIGURES

Death is difficult to define except in negative terms, such as the absence of respiration and heartbeat (*clinical death*), absence of brain functioning (*brain death*), or cessation of organs' functioning (*biological death*). Other definitions of death have focused on what in human experience it might resemble, such as sleep, coma, or a state of virtually no activity. The full experience of death is of course out of the experience of living, which may well make its definition incomplete and contribute to the fear, concerns, and difficulties we have talking about death.

Death among the Elderly

To be old is to be faced with death, whether it is one's own or the death of a spouse or of friends. Six percent of all elderly and approximately one-fifth of the "old old," those over 85, die each year. Younger persons do not always appreciate how well their older relatives have coped with the deaths of others and how well they may be prepared for their own deaths. Research has found that, in the aggregate, older persons are no more afraid of death than younger persons.

The most common causes of death in the elderly are heart disease, cancer, strokes, influenza and pneumonia, arteriosclerosis, accidents, bronchitis, cirrhosis of the liver, and kidney infections. Heart, cancer, and stroke-related conditions account for almost 75 percent of all deaths of the elderly. In addition, Alzheimer's disease may be one of the leading causes of death in the elderly, but its exact influence (both direct and indirect) has not been established at this point.

Most people die in institutions, only 30 percent of deaths taking place in the home. In addition, up to 30 percent of medical care of the elderly is spent during the last twelve months of life, which suggests that we are at least administratively committed to delaying death as a matter of policy.

When older people are asked about their fears related to dying, they list seven types:

Fear of pain
Fear of loss of control
Interruption of goals
Fear of others' deaths
Fear of not being
Fear of punishment in afterlife
Fear for survivors

Frequently, these fears are not stated clearly and may not be in the awareness of the person who has them. Instead, they will be expressed by avoidance of discussions about dying, denial that there is any problem, and demanding or otherwise defensive behavior. These underlying fears can, however, be decreased if they are appropriately identified by family or health professionals.

Stages of Death

As social scientists and others have begun to examine the death process, there has been an attempt to define a specific set of stages or steps one goes through in preparing to die. Elisabeth Kübler-Ross, in her classic book, *On Death and Dying*, theorized that there were five stages one could go through in preparing for death:

Denial: An initial response to finding out that one is dying, characterized by verbalizations that, for example, there must be a mistake in the diagnosis. This stage may have some value in allowing the individual to marshal other psychological resources.

Anger: Next, the dying person may express resentment toward the living, the physician, the rest of the family, friends, and even God. This anger is really a projection of the internal struggle the dying person faces.

Bargaining: In this stage, the dying person attempts to postpone death psychologically by trying to "make a deal" with God to postpone death or pain by promising "good" behavior. If the effort seems successful, another bargain may be attempted.

Depression: As time goes on, the dying person experiences a sense of grief related to physical losses and becomes depressed. The depression, when focused on the future loss of loved ones, is a key move in coming to grips with one's death and may be an important step toward the fifth stage.

Acceptance: In this stage, the dying person has come to grips with his or her mortality and has a full understanding of his or her death. There is a lack of depression and a sense of quietness and calmness about the person who has accepted death.

The stages of death are a useful way for us to appreciate what the dying person may be going through. At the same time, they can be used inappropriately to label our parents, thus dismissing their pain, or be viewed as a series of steps everyone has to go through to have a "good death."

Serious doubts have been raised as to whether or not there are stages, whether the depression at the end of life is a true depression or simply a lack of energy due to illness (and medication), and whether people progress through stages in any systematic fashion. Most experts dealing with the dying would agree that the dying person goes "in and out" of stages, feelings, and concerns. Almost all would also agree that in some cases the dying person is "ready" to die, that he or she has accepted death and is not dying in a great deal of distress or fear.

The question of spiritual concerns is also an important one in considering the death of your parents. In my experience, it is rare (but does happen occasionally) that a dying person returns to the faith if he or she has not been an active participant in organized religion. However, some people have a deep sense of faith that is a great comfort to them as they prepare to die. Others seem equally "ready" without a strong sense of religiousness.

PURPOSES IN TALKING ABOUT DEATH AND DYING

Giving Information

One of the purposes of talking about death and dying with your parents is to give them information. The information may be emotionally laden (as when you discuss a terminal diagnosis or tell them that a spouse, a child, or a friend has died). It may be appear to be more mundane, as in telling your parent that you have asked for assistance in caring for him or her at home because of terminal illness. Also, it may be legal in content, such as giving information about wills and burial information.

At the same time, each bit of information is potentially charged with high emotion and may not be understood. You will need time to let your parents digest what you are telling them, both to work through any emotional reactions and to decide how to use the information.

Talking about Feelings and Reactions

There is general agreement that many persons who are dying want to talk about their death and that talking about it is one way to finish unfinished business, to finalize plans, to review one's life, or make peace with others.

Talking with the dying person can mean sitting quietly, sharing a joke, talking about the weather or news events or family affairs. Talking about feelings does not necessarily mean directly addressing every feeling that comes to mind. Overall, the sense of willingness to listen, share, and care will be more important than the specific ways you go about dealing with the feelings you and your parent have about death, whether it's theirs, a friend's, or relative's.

Family members feel different sets of feelings along the trajectory of death and may be going through their own stages or phases of anticipatory grieving. If you are the child of a dying parent, you may be angry, deny that anything is wrong, attempt to bargain, be depressed about what is happening, or have come to grips with it. You are likely to go "in and out" of the situation.

Even more important, your feelings may not match those of your older parent at a moment in time. Your emotional reactions may be quite different from theirs as you talk about the past, present, and future.

If things are hard, remember that your job is to listen and be the best ear and source of support you can; by so doing, you will be taking care of important business for yourself, for your children, and for your parent. It is perfectly acceptable for you both to cry, to laugh, and even to disagree or fight (without blame) as you would at other times. You may also find that the impact of a pending death is so great that you need to talk with professionals (clergy, mental health professionals, physicians) about your pain.

Discussing the Diagnosis: To Tell or Not to Tell

Timothy was the 92-year-old father of Dee. Timothy had had a good relationship with Dee through the years, but had told her upon occasion that if he ever had a terminal condition, he did not want to know about it. So, when he was diagnosed as having liver cancer, Dee was adamant that he not be told. Timothy suffered as did Dee, who had him move in with her and her family. A few days before he died, she broke down in front of him and cried. When he asked what was troubling her, she said, "Dad, I couldn't tell you, but it wouldn't be right not to. You have a serious disease."

"I know," he replied. "I won't be here much longer."

"I thought you didn't want to know," she said, tears still in her eyes."

"I didn't for a long time," he replied, "but I know after all."

After this discussion, they were able to talk about his funeral arrangements, as well as how he wanted to spend his few remaining days.

I have spent a fair amount of time with two home-based hospice teams over the past several years, consulting with them on issues in patient care. Many times, the family has requested that the patient not be told he or she was dying. In almost every case, the family felt bad about the decision, and, if the patient was not eventually told the truth, there was a sense that things did not work out for the best. As was the case for Pat and Adeline at the beginning of this chapter, the patient frequently knows something is going on and is bewildered by the subtle changes in how others are communicating with him or her.

In many cases, such as that of Timothy and Dee, when the family finally decided to tell the patient he or she was dying, there was great relief all around. More older persons need to be told about their condition honestly and directly (and with compassion and care). Usually it is the family members' problems (as opposed to the older person's) that underlie a decision not to tell.

At the same time, under certain circumstances individuals prefer not to know about their condition or act with such rage and denial that others choose to limit or withhold information. If you choose to withhold information, be sure that your decision is based on your parent's needs (as opposed as to your own). In addition, pay attention to changes in your parent's openness to hearing the information so that you can give it if he or she changes, as Timothy did.

Beyond telling your parents difficult news, your talking with them when they are terminally ill has other important purposes. By being congruent and relating to them as persons, you are helping them *live* their last days instead of *die* their last days. Many of the fears mentioned above can be dispelled, in part, by reassurance (not false reassurance) that you care, that there is hope, that some things can be done to make them comfortable, and that they count. You can also be a listener, which will not always be easy. You will be listening to your mother's or father's pain, hurts, sad memories, grief at leaving this world, and other issues that you can do little about except listen.

Dying with Dignity

One of the great lessons that have been learned from people who work with the dying is that there are specific things that can be done to improve the quality of life for the dying person. These are all subsumed under the idea of "death with dignity." By this, I mean that the dying person has the right to

- Privacy
- Control over as much of his or life as possible (including when to get up, when and what to eat, what clothes to wear, what activities to do, what topics to discuss)
- Make decisions
- Decide whether or not to discuss his or her death at a given moment
- Decide whom he or she wants to talk with (including spouse, children, health professionals, clergy, and/or friends)
- Have any wishes granted by others, within the limitations of resources and the dying person's condition

The only way to learn what most of the above mean to your parents is to find out directly, that is, to talk and listen to what is said. Wishes may not be articulated well, and some may be hard to request (such as not wanting to talk to a child or spouse). You can do a world of good for your parents by being supportive of their wishes and encouraging them to be frank with you, remembering at the same time that you need to be nonjudgmental about what they might say and able to listen to discomforting feelings or concerns.

Talking about the Death of Others

Another purpose in discussing death and dying is talking with your parent about the death of others, such as a spouse, your sisters or brothers, or friends your parents have known. While there is no question that some persons live in their grief for an inordinate period of time, remember that it can take more than a year for people to go through the grieving process. One of the things to be careful of is to be around to give support after the immediate weeks following a death when others, including family and friends, have effectively left the scene.

Widowhood deserves at least a short mention in this context. More than half of the older women in the United States are widows. Widows are significantly poorer, have less adequate housing, lower status, less active social lives, and worse physical health than married women. In addition, widowhood still has a stigma attached to it. Despite the existence of some cultural roles for widows, there is often a sense that social activities are planned for couples and/or families, but not for the "fifth wheel" or the "third person." Widows are also frequently torn between getting their own lives in order and somehow being "faithful" to the memory of a spouse.

Any of these issues may warrant some attention from you, or you may feel that a support service or professional is needed to talk to a parent who has faced the death of a spouse or close relative or friend. The books and resources mentioned at the end of this chapter may be of help to you if you are unsure about how to proceed.

Talking about Plans

Another reason to talk about death is to help your parent make plans, including funeral arrangements and drawing up (or updating) a will. Several strong emotional currents are involved in discussing these matters while a person is dying. At the same time, if they are not discussed (by either you or a professional), your parent's wishes may not come to pass after his or her death.

Learning about Your Parents and Yourself

An issue related to talking about plans is to begin to discuss death with your parents at the earliest time you can, preferably before a crisis hits. While it is difficult and scary to talk about dying "out of the blue," once the topic has been discussed by both of you, it is considerably easier to talk about it again. Also, in talking about death, you are accepting the process of dying as a part of life, rather than pretending that it doesn't happen, should not be discussed, and is better off avoided.

RESPONSES OF THE ELDERLY

Ramona had cancer and was likely to die within a year. She was 82 and lived with her sister. On a visit to her house, I spent time talking with her about her condition, her life, and her future. She was happy that the family was getting together at one son's house for Christmas. When I asked her if her family knew she had cancer, she said, "I don't want them to know. I know I have cancer and I know what that means."

Further conversation brought out that she had cared for her mother, who had had cancer twenty years previously and died a painful death. Actually, with new advances in pain management, that was not at all the way things had to be for Ramona. A conversation with Ramona's son indicated that he already knew about her condition but, like his mother, was afraid to talk about it because he "knew" how painful cancer was.

You may find any of a range of responses from your own parent when topics related to death are raised. There may be a closing off or a quick change of topic. There could be denial ("There's nothing wrong" or "I'll get this thing licked" or the search for a miracle cure from unreliable physicians and others), anger, depression, withdrawal, or blaming others for the problem.

In addition, be prepared for strong emotions to surface for both of you, particularly if your discussions take place for the first time while your parent, his or her spouse, or a family member is dying. Be prepared to share, to talk, to touch, to hug.

Also, family myths about death and the condition have to be handled carefully. In the case of Ramona, both she and her son were trying to protect each other. However, without identifying their commonly held myth, there could be little communication between them about her condition.

At the same time, many older persons handle their death or the death of others with acceptance, compassion, and great humanity. The emotional support of family can only aid the process of dying to be an integral part of life.

Gail, 78, had been a widow for seven years. She had cancer of the liver and had only a few weeks to live. Her family was very close to her. Gail also had a boyfriend, Wendall, who was a widower. Gail lived with her daughter, Marcia, and son-in-law, Harvey. On New Year's eve, Marcia and Harvey wanted to go out but could not leave Gail alone. After some discussion with Gail, Marcia suggested picking Wendall up and bringing him over to the house for the evening while Marcia and Harvey went out. A good time was had by all.

In this case, the family was able to help Gail enjoy her last days without denying the severity of her condition. There is a lot the rest of us can learn from families like Gail's.

INFORMATION NEEDED

If you have to talk with your parents about their having a terminal illness, it makes good sense to have appropriate background information, including the diagnosis, how the disease might progress, and answers to questions that may be asked, including how much pain, discomfort, and disfigurement there may be. You should consult with the attending physician or another professional connected with your parent's case. In addition, clergy are becoming quite sophisticated in psychological issues about death and dying. You can also consult with them, nursing staff, social workers, or others involved in the care of your parent to obtain medical and other information you need.

If you are discussing plans, it would be useful to know what the options are for wills, as well as funeral arrangements and, of course, the cultural and religious rituals of your particular family. You may also want to do some reading about how people cope with death to give you a general sense of what to expect from the dying person as well as how others have dealt with death in their families. Several of the books listed at the end of this chapter are useful in this regard.

STEPS, STRATEGIES, TIME, AND TIMING

Vanessa's father, Walter, age 89, had incurable lung cancer. He had had treatment at the beginning of the disease, but it had failed. Nevertheless, Walter denied that he was sick and continually talked about what he would do when he got better.

This pained Vanessa as well as Nancy, Walter's wife. They met with the physician who was monitoring Walter's case, who suggested to them to follow Walter's lead as to when to talk to him about the reality of his condition. After a few weeks, Walter began to give hints that all was not right with him. He began to talk with Nancy and with his daughter. Some days he wanted to talk, others he did not.

Vanessa had to learn how to react to the way her father was feeling on a given day and then be supportive and follow his lead. The steps and strategies below all reflect this basic approach to talking with the dying.

- Pay attention to your parents' lead. That is, appreciate their attempts to talk as well as their hints that it is not the time to talk.

- Pay attention to your own feelings and reactions, and be prepared to talk about them as well as information and the task at hand.
- Be careful about the differences between reassurance and false reassurance.
- While it may not be possible to talk directly about matters that concern you, because of either your own difficulty in talking about them or your parents' expected (and real) reaction, you can begin to approach the issue by asking questions like "Is this a good time to talk about it?" or "Do you want to talk about it now?"
- If your parents refuse to talk, keep the door open to raise the subject another time. If you have gotten a strong refusal to talk about the issue, including the familiar "I don't want to talk about it" response, you can leave the door open to raising the question again by saying things such as "Let's leave it for today"; "We'll talk about it when we're both ready"; or "I want to talk about it, but I will wait until you are ready," followed by asking, a while or a day or so later, "Is this a good time to talk about it?" The key issue in these strategies is that you are accepting the refusal but you are not accepting its finality. This makes sense because we know that people go through different sets of reactions at various times (or, if you accept them, stages of going through death).
- Touch, empathy, and active listening are very important. At times the people surrounding a dying person act as if he or she has already left this world, avoiding discussion and physical contact. Remember that the dying person needs compassion and constant reminders that he or she is still alive and has the opportunity to talk about what she or he is feeling.
- If you are at a loss for how to begin your discussion, ask one of the following:
    "What do *you* want to talk about today?"
    "What do *you* want for yourself today?"
    (With compassion) "What can I do for you today?"
- Talk with other family members, including your children. Everyone will benefit from the opportunity to have their feelings and reactions shared and appreciated. In the case of Vanessa and Nancy above, it was important for the two of them to be in contact, but also it allowed Nancy to be supportive of Vanessa's discussions with her father rather

than feel left out or hurt if Walter would only talk to Vanessa on a given day.

OUTCOMES

Most of the outcomes of your discussions of death and dying will focus on feelings. However, if you are addressing issues in planning or making arrangements for funerals or wills, then you should take a hard look at what steps need to happen next and who is going to do them.

WHAT YOU WANT TO SAY, WHAT YOU CAN LIVE WITH SAYING

Given the subjective nature of talking about death, much of what you want to say or can live with saying depends on you and, equally important, on your parents. You will have to weigh the nature of the circumstances facing your parents and your needs and theirs to decide what you want to say and what you have to say.

HOW TO KNOW YOU'RE IN TROUBLE—AND THEN WHAT?

In discussions about death and dying, it is hard to know whether you're in trouble or simply going through difficult feelings. At the least, if you begin to feel overwhelmed, more frightened than you are comfortable being, or find yourself dreading what happens next, you may be heading in the wrong direction.

Paradoxically, you may also be in trouble if everything is going *too* smoothly, in that the painful parts are being glossed over or denied. In either case, some regrouping is needed, whether by spending time alone, stopping the conversation, focusing on feelings, calling someone else in to help you and your parent, or discussing matters with the nurse, physician, mental health professional or clergy member who may be involved in the situation.

RESOURCES

There have been a substantial number of excellent works written about aspects of death and dying. The following four are a good sample of available books on the topic.

Kastenbaum, R. S. *Death, Society, and Human Experience*. 2nd ed. St. Louis: C. V. Mosby Co., 1981. This is more of a textbook than others cited here, but it covers a wide range of issues related to death and dying in a manner that is both caring and informative.

Kübler-Ross, E. *On Death and Dying*. New York: Macmillan, 1969. Dr. Kübler-Ross has also written numerous other books and articles on this topic. This is the classic book on stages of death and how talking about it helps the dying person.

Kushner, H. S. *When Bad Things Happen to Good People*. New York: Schocken Books, 1981. Addresses issues of religion and death in an eloquent manner.

Veninga, R. *A Gift of Hope: How We Survive Our Tragedies*. Boston: Little, Brown & Co., 1985. Focusing on grief and other issues related to loss, this book addresses both practical and personal issues for survivors.

There are many hospice organizations throughout the United States that are focused on the care of the terminally ill. Being in a hospice program means options for home care, many professionals being involved, and having volunteers available. Write the following address or look up "Hospice Programs" in the Yellow Pages.

National Hospice Organization
1901 N. Fort Meyer Drive, Suite 400
Arlington, VA 22209
(703) 243-5900)

Other organizations offer widow-to-widow services or specific counseling for the bereaved and/or dying. Contact your local church, synagogue, United Way, hospice, mental health center, or social service organizations to find names of appropriate organizations in your area.

13
Talking about Nursing Homes
and Long-Term Care

Barbara was the daughter-in-law of Myrna, age 79. Myrna's husband, Jack, had died three years earlier in a nursing home. Barbara's husband, Andrew, had been close to his parents and insisted that his mother move in with him and Barbara after his father's death.

All went well for the first two years. Barbara, however, was beginning to feel trapped. Myrna, along with being demanding and then denying that she was demanding, was beginning to lose control over urination, had fallen a few times, and was coming out of a hospital in two weeks after a hip replacement operation. Myrna also seemed to need constant assistance because of her difficulties walking and transferring to the toilet in the home. Barbara found that she could not give any time to her teenage children and had to quit a part-time job, even though she and Andrew needed the money for their children's looming college educations.

All through this time, Andrew insisted that they take care of his mother at home. Finally, one evening, he admitted to Barbara that he had made a "deathbed" promise to his father that Myrna would never go to a nursing home. It was only after considerable discussion with each other, with a counselor, and finally with Myrna (who, it turned out, expected to go to a nursing home earlier) that Andrew overcame his guilt and arranged what was, for all of them, a sensible placement in a nearby facility.

The staffs of virtually every nursing home I have visited have told me this story: An older woman, who had health problems that warranted placement in a nursing home, was never told that her children were considering placing her. Rather, one day, she was told that she was going for a "visit" to a facility. (Or, in variation of this story, after a hospitalization, a woman is told she is going to spend a few days or weeks in the nursing home.) The children dropped her off, and, to her growing surprise, every day when she asked, "When am I going home?," she could not get a straight answer. The family were then absent or, when they did visit, were very guilty, finding fault with the staff and the facility, as they waited for their relative to adapt to the new surroundings.

These two stories illustrate some of the common dilemmas facing children who have to discuss nursing homes and other forms of long-term care with their parents: promises, obligations, and guilt combine to make these discussions painful for all concerned. However, if the issues, as painful as they are, are avoided, the guilt, pain, and discomfort will only grow and positive changes are unlikely to take place.

Nursing homes are one of the most feared places for many older persons. While some of the fears have to do with horror stories that occasionally surface, fears are more related to what being in a nursing home may represent: loss of independence, being "left to die," regimentation, "being with all those old folks," or "going senile."

Both the process of deciding upon institutionalization and how all involved handle it and subsequent visits and contact are the focus of this chapter. These discussions are also related to talking about using other forms of long-term care services, some of which are described below.

FACTS AND FIGURES

Contrary to popular belief, only 5 percent of the elderly live in institutional settings. The vast majority are on their own. At the same time, the odds are that 25 percent of the elderly will spend some time in a nursing home, even if it is a short-term stay to recover from an operation or illness.

Nursing homes evolved from old people's homes and veterans' homes after the two world wars. The advent of Medicare in 1965 created the nursing home industry as it is known today, as people found that they could make money caring for the frail elderly, thanks to government reimbursement for certain types of care, primarily medical. Nursing home care has gone from 1 percent of the nation's health-care dollars in the 1960s to well over 5 percent of its health-care dollars at present, two-thirds of which come from public sources, primarily Medicaid. One of the facts of life is that nursing home patients who go in as private paying patients (which can cost between $25,000 and $30,000 a year) frequently deplete their resources over time and then have to go on public assistance.

Types of Nonresidential Long-Term Care

Adult Day Care. Adult day care provides structured programs for "frail" elderly who live at home but come to a facility for structured activities.

Adult day care centers have grown rapidly throughout the country. They may have a medical, social, or even psychological focus, although many share common objectives. There are usually several staff members working with older persons who are brought to the setting for socializing, some therapeutic activities, and as a way to relieve families of full-time care of their relatives and enable them to work and carry on other aspects of their lives. Adult day care centers are not federally licensed or certified, although some states are moving in the direction of certification.

Respite Care. Respite care, a relatively new idea, involves programs that either place trained helpers in a home to provide companionship and a break for family members or provide beds in a hospital or nursing home to give full-time family caregivers time away from their relative for a needed rest or vacation.

Types of Full-Time Long-Term Care

Group Homes. Group homes are settings in which several older persons live, having their meals and laundry provided by the home operator but otherwise on their own. Group homes may be licensed and/or eligible for some reimbursement, depending on their type and state law.

Intermediate-Care Facilities. An intermediate-care facility is either self-standing or part of a long-term care (nursing home) facility. Intermediate care means that the older person is capable of some activities and does not need extensive nursing care and close supervision. Decisions as to eligibility depend on state laws and physician determination. Persons in intermediate care are considered ill enough to receive certain benefits from insurance, including Medicaid.

Skilled Nursing Care. Skilled nursing care is designed for the individual who is in need of complex nursing and medical services. As is the case for intermediate care, a physician's decision and the fulfillment of certain state and federal requirements are necessary to designate a person as eligible for skilled care. Both skilled and intermediate patients' progress and eligibility for public funding (including Medicare) are periodically reviewed in each facility. In addition, individual facilities may be non-profit, profitmaking (there are actually several large national chains of nursing homes), or, less frequently, municipal.

Some Facts about Nursing Home Residents

Nursing homes may seem sterile, isolated, and depressing to many people. Some of the reactions we have to these settings are due to our expectations, some are related to their being institutions (that is, living situations in which others have total control and responsibility for one's well-being), and some may be reactions to what nursing homes represent to us. The following facts should help you sort out some of your reactions to the idea of institutionalizing a parent or other older relative.

Nursing home residents frequently have several chronic conditions. More than half of them need help bathing; more than half need help walking. Their average age is 80 years; the vast majority are female, widowed, and poor. There is a belief that the process of going into an institution results in a higher mortality rate, although it seems that voluntary institutionalization (that is, the resident is a participant in the decision) is much less disruptive and life-threatening than involuntary institutionalization.

Experts have raised the question of how many persons in institutions could be managed at home if there were adequate support services. Estimates run between 10 and 30 percent. However, there are frequently not enough home-based services, funds to pay for such services (from insurance companies and the government) are more limited, and families have to carry the brunt of time and management of the services. One emerging trend in this area is the development of private case management groups, professionals who help families orchestrate care for older persons at home, including some long-term options, such as respite care and adult day care.

Another fact of life in nursing homes is that the bulk of dollars are spent on medical concerns and aspects of safety. Issues related to the quality of life are given a lower financial priority, so that nursing home administrators can find it difficult to have comprehensive programming for residents. Facilities with historical and cultural ties to their communities (such as municipal nursing homes, church-related homes, or Jewish homes for the elderly), frequently have an interested and motivated group of volunteers and cultural programming available.

Also, the conditions that lead to persons living in long-term care settings are difficult for them and others around them. A large portion of residents are likely to have some signs of depression, and many are confused. At the same time, people who have worked in these settings have found that in many cases the human spirit of the residents is capable of being lifted and ignited. Much of the depression and some of the confusion can be lifted by an interesting environment and meaningful activities. Social events such as "happy hours" (complete with wine) and even sheltered workshops have been successful in some settings.

Given the issues, meanings of institutionalization, stigma, and historic problems associated with nursing homes, it is not surprising that they are frequently viewed as undesirable by older persons and families. Persons in the nursing home industry feel they are victims of unfair stereotypes, which is, in part, true. At the same time, the prospect of having an older person move from his or her own house to a more regimented setting (even if it is cleaner, better for his or her health, and safer) is potentially painful for everyone. Families and older persons frequently feel guilt, anger, remorse, and a sense of failure in having to be faced with institutionalization. Because of these overriding feelings, it is particularly important to understand your purposes in talking with your parents about long-term care, appreciate both their and your own responses to the issue, find out relevant information ahead of the time you will need it, and have sound strategies for discussing these concerns.

PURPOSES, RESPONSES, INFORMATION NEEDED, AND STRATEGIES

Because of the likelihood of guilt, a sense of failed obligation, and misunderstanding, you need to carefully consider your purpose in talking with your parent about institutionalization or other forms of long-term care.

Preparing Your Parent for Institutionalization

Stanley, a highly educated engineer, was the dutiful son of Jane, who was in her mid-seventies. Stanley knew that his mother's arthritis was so bad that she could no longer walk and that institutionalization was the best answer. He had discussed it with her, and she had agreed that it was a good idea. The best facility in the area was a church home that had between a six- and twelve-month waiting list. Stanley got his mother's name on the list. When it came time for her to visit, they went, took the tour, and answered the questions. As they were leaving the home, Jane turned to Stanley and said, "I could never live here."

After Stanley's initial shock at Jane's response, it took months of discussion (specifically reviewing the visit and allowing Jane to talk about her reactions), listening, and patience for Jane to finally decide that she was going to move into a nursing home. While the decision took considerable time from Stanley's point of view, when it finally happened, Jane had little difficulty adjusting to the change in her life.

This story highlights several of the issues involved in the process of talking about institutionalization. Like Stanley and Jane, most persons find themselves talking about nursing homes with their parents after a crisis or series of events has taken place that makes the decision virtually inevitable. This type of discussion is difficult on all sides, as frequently there has been little preparation and in all likelihood little inclusion of the older person in the family's deliberations.

This type of discussion is not easy to begin, nor is it easy to hear some of the likely responses from your parent, which may include a mixture of grieving for lost independence, fear about what going to a nursing home means, and some distrust of others. At the same time, remember that when you raise the issue, it will be the first time your parent may have discussed it with anyone. You are likely to be ahead of him or her in your thoughts, as you may have had several discussions with health professionals and nursing home administrators as well as other family.

This discussion will go best if it is done early and includes your parent in the decisions. Much like Stanley, you may have to to weather storms of anger, frustration, fear, and refusal before moving on to other aspects that are worthy of discussion, including issues of maintaining a household, putting valuables in a safe place, what items to bring to a new residence, and so forth.

One of the key issues here is allowing enough time for the issues to sink in and for your parent to respond, rather than timing the discussion so that you do not have to listen to what may be difficult. If you are prepared for it, you will do better to hear what has to be said rather than letting any issues with you continue to build up and be vented on others.

Shopping for a Facility

Robert and Noreen were looking at several facilities for their mother, Agnes, who went with them for each visit. Agnes was quiet and lethargic, but Robert and Noreen both knew that she was taking everything in. They had discussed the pending institutionalization with Agnes, who felt depressed about the issue but agreed with them that this was the best option for her. They also had prepared a checklist of things they wanted to look at in a facility and mentally took notes at each visit.

One of the facilities they went to was highly recommended by several friends, including a nurse and social worker who worked in community agencies. When they went in for an initial visit, however, the administrator ignored Agnes and invited Robert and Noreen into his office, suggesting that they leave Agnes outside in a waiting area, as "She does not really have to hear all of this, now, does she?"

After the discussion, Robert and Noreen left the facility knowing they would never place their mother there.

Robert and Noreen are one example of how a family seriously approached the possibility of institutional placement. They planned ahead, included their mother in the planning, and paid attention to how they were *all* treated by potential residences for their mother.

If you are talking about looking at facilities, you would also do well to talk about what you think the important aspects of choosing a nursing home are. Several resources in this area are listed at the end of this chapter. Some key points to consider are:

- Recommendations by others, including clergy, hospital staff, friends, and physicians
- Cleanliness (including no offensive smells)
- Level of activity and activity options that fit your parent's interests and abilities (You may also want to consider how the facility handles persons suffering from confusion in case your parent becomes confused during his or her stay there.)
- Willingness of administration and staff to talk with you as a potential customer
- Willingness of administration to include your parent as a full member of the decision team. Although it is not always a predictor of troubles later on, if the administrator (or whoever meets with you) talks to your parent as if he or she were a child, I suggest that you put that particular facility near the bottom of your list.
- Ease and flexibility of visiting hours
- Willingness to allow items of "sentimental" value in individuals' rooms
- Availability of resident government and resident-initiated activities (a sign that residents are encouraged to be more than simply "patients")

- Evidence that relatively few residents sit in hallways without much to do
- Dining facilities and availability of alternate menus
- Outside affiliations with community, church, and volunteer groups
- Policy on residents going out to visit family overnight
- Certification of the facility for Medicare and Medicaid (Also, if your parent changes status from private paying to Medicaid-supported, would there be any change in room assignment or any other status change?)

There are other important guidelines to consider, many of which are spelled out in detail in the references at the end of this chapter.

Even after several visits, your parent may not want to live in any of the places you have seen for good reasons, namely all the reasons institutions are not likable. If that is the case, you have another mission and purpose, as discussed in the next section.

Helping Your Parent Adapt to a Tough Decision

Michelle, 92, was the oldest member of her family. Her children and sisters had been worried about her for some time, as she was legally blind, had diabetes and severe arthritis, and probably had Alzheimer's disease. However, she had no interest in a nursing home, denying that she had any need for help. Finally, her sisters persuaded her to go to a facility "for a few weeks" while her daughter, Victoria, was on vacation. Everyone in the family except Michelle knew that Michelle's placement was permanent.

Victoria spent her entire vacation with her family worrying about what to tell her mother when she returned, as Michelle kept asking the staff and her own sisters, "When will I go back home?"

In this case, Victoria was faced with "triple jeopardy." First, her mother was misled as to why she was going into the institution, although there was ample reason for misleading her and little that could be done after the family made their decision. Second, it is likely that the rest of the family was upset about Michelle's condition, and worried that the same thing might happen to them (so Victoria could expect all kinds of avoidance, guilt, and fear on their parts). Finally, there was Victoria's guilt over the institutionalization and the way in which it was done.

Each of these issues may need to be addressed and considered before Victoria talks to her mother about what is going on. However, and I want to stress this point, there will be no "getting straight" about what happened unless Victoria and Michelle talk directly (and nondefensively) about it. Even if Michelle seems to "adapt" by being quiet, the odds are that she will be depressed rather than accepting, a tough price to pay for not having a confrontation. In addition, if things are not handled, subsequent visits will exact a huge price on all family members, which could easily result in minimal contact between Michelle and her family.

From a distance, I can only admire the determination to be individ-ualistic, independent, and other attributes that can go into an older person's "stubborn" refusal to enter a nursing home. At the same time, given that such a move is warranted and that the older person is not willing to make it, helping him or her adapt and accept the move *without* giving up hope, identity, and self-esteem are the purposes behind talking to help your parent adapt.

Adaptation does *not* mean resignation or becoming lifeless and de-pressed. It does mean some recognition of the realities of a situation as well as handling the emotional reactions to the situation.

Adaptation also can mean finding the best way to keep up one's interest, motivation, and self-esteem while living in an institution. This may not be easy. You will have to be prepared to listen without judging (and reacting too strongly) to your parent's airing of feelings of depression, anger, and abandonment. Your listening will be very important in main-taining trust between the two of you.

It can also be frustrating listening to a parent who refuses to make the final decision, like Stanley's mother, Jane. If you can prevent yourself from being overwhelmed, you can provide a valuable service to your parent. You may be in a position of having to push for the decision being made, using an assertive style and focusing on realities and consequences (e.g., "You know you cannot stay where you are—it's too difficult for you to manage the stairs" or "Mom, we care for you, we will care for you, *and* we can't take care of you here").

However, if the decision is *really* to be your parent's (even if it is only the decision *when* to move), you will have to let your parent decide and allow him or her the psychological room to refuse. In my experience, pushing too hard (e.g., by saying, "Mom, you have to move and that's it; I don't want to hear any more of this refusal") actually slows down the older person's adapting to the realities of his or her situation. While the question of how much time to allow for adaptation is critical to think out, it may be that your own need to have the issue settled makes you pressure them to decide or adapt immediately.

Getting Information about Complaints

> Lynne's mother, Bridget, age 83, was a nursing home resident. Lynne would visit two or three times a week. One week, Bridget was very agitated. "They're stealing my things," she cried as her daughter came in. Lynne, who felt guilty about her mother's being in an institution, immediately went to the charge nurse and demanded an explanation. Together, they went back to Bridget's room.
> "What is missing?" asked the nurse.
> "My robe," replied Bridget, still upset. "They're stealing my clothes."
> "When was the last time you remember having it on?" asked the nurse.
> Bridget could not remember. Lynne and the nurse looked around the room and could not find it. Then Lynne remembered that Bridget had said something about having a fever the previous day. "Mom," she asked, "did anyone help you when you had the fever?"
> "Yes, someone came in and took my wet things off."
> Lynne and the nurse went into the bathroom and to everyone's relief found the robe hung up and drying out.

Another reason for talking to your parent about nursing homes is to hear his or her complaints about the place. Nursing home residents may complain about food, how they are treated (bathed, handled), having their possessions disappear (usually describing them as "stolen" even if they turn up in the laundry room), and other issues that suggest mistreatment. Some of the charges are true, some have different explanations than the ones given by the resident, and some are more a symbolic reaction to a particular room, particular staff members, the resident's physical or mental condition, or even simply being in an institution in the first place.

If you are faced with such complaints, filter them through your own sense of what is accurate, how you view the staff who may be accused, and your own feelings of guilt or responsibility about your parent's care. Avoid taking out your guilt feelings on staff members, who will probably react with resentment.

The first step in finding out the truth in these matters is talking to your parent to obtain more information. You will probably have to ask questions about the when, where, and what of the complaint. In the case above, instead of demanding a solution to the "problem," Lynne could have obtained some information and then discussed it with the nurse, with much better "public relations" as a result.

Your parent may take your questioning to mean you do not trust or believe him or her. If so, you should be reassuring but at the same time make your own independent decision about what has happened and what to do. You can assure your parent that you care and believe that this is how things appear to him or her, and that you are going to "get to the bottom of this."

In addition to finding out more about complaints, you should be knowledgeable about the "Patient's Bill of Rights." Each state has to comply with federal standards for patient care, which it can then modify (by giving more protection to patients). Such bills of rights should be posted in a facility and listed as state statutes. You may, if you wish, report complaints about nursing home care to outside agencies, such as public health officials or ombudsmen programs, which also exist in each state, although the form varies. You are, after all, an advocate for your parent and may need to get information from them to pursue a legitimate problem or concern.

Visits

Visits to a nursing home can be disturbing, depressing, and uncomfortable for family members. People tend to feel that the visit will be easier to get through if the conversation is kept light and if nothing of an upsetting nature is talked about.

Nothing is further from the truth. Remember that "report card" visits are probably boring for all parties involved, including your parent. Visits can be an invaluable form of connection between your parent and you and other family members or friends, as well as a link to the outside world in general. Visits are good opportunities to talk about one's life, important events, and concerns your parent may have. By treating the visit as a potentially meaningful interaction, you may have a quite different conversation with your parent than he or she has the rest of the day. Remember, though, that it may take a few minutes for him or her to shift gears from being a patient to being a parent, grandparent, or family member.

If you are bringing other family members for visits, they may need to be prepared for your parent's physical condition, especially if he or she is confined to bed. You may need to help them find ways to relate to the "person" rather than the "condition," as well as block out parts of the environment that are hard for them to handle.

In these visits, it is a good idea to have things to talk about that are meaningful and comfortable for you and your parents, including reminiscence. Talking about the past is natural for older persons. It can bring back pleasant memories and feelings that are absent in current circumstances. At the same time, however, talking about the past does *not* mean pretending or going along with pretending that you are living in the past. In addition, you should not use talking about the past as a way of avoiding talking about important issues facing all of you in the present.

The only way I know to make visiting in a nursing home enjoyable (and it can be) is to make human connections with people who are there, including the use of touch, good eye contact, and arranging the physical setup so that it is easy and comfortable for both of you to see, hear, and touch each other. If the visit is superficial, artificial, and not "connected," chances are that you will find yourself eagerly waiting for the visit to be over, avoiding discussing feelings, and becoming irrelevant, superreasonable, or placating to your parent.

DEVELOPING STRATEGIES FOR TALKING ABOUT NURSING HOMES

Along with the specific strategies discussed above, keep the following issues and approaches in mind as you decide how to talk to your parents about nursing homes or other forms of long-term care.

- *Include your parent and other family members in decisions from the beginning.* Exclusion may make the going easier for a short while, but it will hinder trust and acceptance of changes, and cannot help your relationship.
- *Be specific and truthful.* Avoidance makes the truth more painful to hear later on, as in the case of Laura and Sandy. It also decreases trust and implies that your parent is somehow deficient or needs to be protected from reality, two messages that can hardly raise self-esteem. At the same time, the truth, when put in general statements such as "You cannot take care of yourself," is likely to be heard as a statement about *all* aspects of oneself, which is not true, and as a statement about one's worth, which is not intended. Rather, make specific statements such

as "Your condition means that you need others to be with you all the time" or "It is unsafe for you to be here with the stove because you forget to turn it off" or "Your condition means that you need to have a nurse available all day." These are more truthful and less overgeneralized. Let the reasons for talking about institutionalization be accurate. We do not mean to institutionalize the human spirit, and our discussions should not lead our parents to believe that we want to institutionalize theirs.

- *Use reassurance; avoid false reassurance.* The process of institutionalization is one of loss of identity, of belongings, of choice. You can be of great help by constantly reassuring your parents that you are not emotionally abandoning them, that you feel that the decision is correct (assuming that you do), and that you are maintaining contact. At the same time, avoid giving your parents the false reassurance that they have nothing to worry about, that all is wonderful in the setting, that all the staff care for them all the time, and so forth.

- *Promise only what you can deliver.* When you will visit, what you will bring, whom you will bring, and special outings (taking a resident out for a ride, home for a holiday, and so forth) are promises easily made but not always so easily kept. Sometimes, promises are made out of guilt and then forgotten. Your parents will show amazing retention of them, however, and a promise not kept will hurt more than never making one at all.

- *Talk openly about guilt, obligations, and other uncomfortable topics.* Although there are situations in which opening a discussion about guilt, obligations, and the like will expose you to blame and other negative reactions from your parent, too often we expect these reactions and almost *make* them happen because of our defensive attitude. If this is an area that you are unsure about, consult with appropriate staff in a nursing home, including nursing, social services, and recreation, as to how to raise these topics with your parents. You will, of course, have to evaluate how sophisticated and "on the money" they are about your parent. You may also want to consult with professionals outside of the facility for ideas on how to talk about these topics.

OUTCOMES, WHAT YOU HAVE TO SAY, WHAT YOU CAN LIVE WITH SAYING

There are three types of outcome to consider in talking about nursing homes or other forms of long-term care: having your parents become educated about and prepared for the need for services; having them decide to make the change; and adapting to the change. Of these, adaptation will take longest, making the change may have to take place under circumstances that are not optimal, and education may be avoided because it will not be seen as preparing for an inevitable circumstance.

In each of these areas, there will be some latitude as to what you have to say and what you can live with saying. Inasmuch as you can decrease (or hold in check) your guilt about "failing" or being a "bad child," or otherwise disturbing your sense of self-worth, you can be of better help to your parent in talking about and then taking action about the need for a nursing home or other forms of long-term care.

RESOURCES

Cohen, D., and C. Eisdorfer. *The Loss of Self*. New York: W. W. Norton, 1986. Chapter 10, "Choosing a Nursing Home If the Time Comes," is an excellent selection for further background information.

Silverstone, B., and H. K. Hyman. *You and Your Aging Parents*. Mount Vernon, N.Y.: Consumers Union, 1982. Both the section on nursing homes and Appendix C (a checklist for evaluating a nursing home) are useful.

National Citizen's Coalition for Nursing Home Reform, a private organization, is based in Washington and has developed good literature on choosing nursing homes and handling the myriad issues facing family members. Its address is 1424 16th Street N.W., Suite L-2, Washington, DC 20036.

Many states have ombudsman programs, with specific persons investigating nursing home complaints. Contact your local area agency on aging to see if such a program is in effect in your area.

14

Talking about Family Matters

Bill visits his mother every Sunday. They talk about many things, including politics, city affairs, and other family members. Bill knows that his sister, Sabrina, and his mother do not get along. His mother rarely mentions Sabrina, but when she does, she makes a sarcastic comment or puts Sabrina in a bad light. Bill feels uncomfortable being part of this kind of discussion but does not know what to do about it, so he sits quietly and waits for the topic to change.

Lorry is the middle-aged child of Donald and Collette. Every year, Lorry and her family have gone to her parents' house for Thanksgiving dinner. This year, however, Lorry's husband's family is having a large family reunion on Thanksgiving Day. Lorry has put off telling her parents about the change in plans because she does not know how to tell them without hurting their feelings.

Brandy's cousin Rosa was getting a divorce. Brandy knew that her own mother, Tracey, was adamantly opposed to divorce. Yet Brandy decided to tell Tracey about the divorce since she was in close contact with Rosa's family.

When Brandy spoke to her mother, she made sure that they had an hour for discussion, which allowed her mother to talk about how awful divorce was and whose fault it was and so forth. In addition, Brandy told Tracey that she also felt bad about the divorce, but that Rosa needed all the support she could get from family, as this was a tough time for her; that Rosa did not go into the marriage wanting to be divorced; and that Tracey might really hurt Rosa by blaming or rejecting her when they talked.

Each of these situations focuses on an aspect of talking about families. Bill was in the position of struggling with taking sides versus confronting his mother and was caught in several roadblocks, like trying to get parental approval and not knowing how to avoid arguments. Lorry was faced with changing a family norm, feet guilty about doing it, and did not appreciate the value of early assertion and focusing on specifics. Brandy, on the other hand, used several strategies to prime her mother to be supportive of Rosa, including giving her time to vent, focusing on consequences of behavior such as blame, and talking about feelings.

These cases also illustrate some of the circumstances under which family issues arise. As discussed below, the family is an important part of an older person's life. Talking about the family is also an issue that will intrude into discussions of finances, housing, health, and other topics in this book.

FACTS AND FIGURES

Despite myths to the contrary, old persons are not abandoned by their families. Most have weekly contact with family members, although the encounters are more likely to be "social chats" than meaningful discussions. Many older persons have children within a one hour's travel time. Over 80 percent of the needs for assistance that older persons have are met by family members, including shopping, financial support, chores, companionship, and long-term care needs.

When an older person needs help, in many families one person becomes the designated caregiver. This person is most often the spouse, then a daughter or daughter-in-law, then a son or other relative. Most caregivers are women. Families vary considerably in how much they are involved in decisions and shouldering financial and emotional aspects of caregiving. In part, competing obligations, family norms, and family rules about who does what will determine who takes care of an older relative, who is included in decisions, and who shoulders financial responsibility.

One changing reality is that caregivers may have their roles for many years, such as a woman who takes care of an incapacitated spouse or a parent with Alzheimer's disease. Some of the research that has been done at the University of Bridgeport in Connecticut, as well as other places, suggests that nearly one-third of working women over the age of 40 are already caregivers to dependent older relatives. One of the more startling demographic facts is that by the end of the century, for every person between the ages of 65 and 75, there will be another person over the age of 75, which means that we will be caring for older relatives well into our retirement years.

On the other side of the coin, elderly parents are frequently sources of support for their adult children. For example, some research suggests that older parents give aid as well as receive it, although the amount of aid (which can be financial as well as emotional, or services such as baby-sitting) may diminish as parents age. One interesting study showed that parents were the most important source of support for middle-aged widows, more so than friends or children.

Most children and older parents report positive feelings about each other. Some relationships are primarily negative, and others are a mixture of positive and negative feelings.

Most older persons have living brothers or sisters. It is not uncommon for siblings in old age to try to reestablish or improve contact, make efforts to visit, and rely on each other in time of need.

The role of grandparent is less firmly established than other familial roles. While there are different cultural norms, the specific tasks that go with being a grandparent are not well defined by culture or race, although there are likely to be clear norms in your own family.

One other fact deserves mention. Older parents are important persons in their children's lives. Similarly, children are important persons in their parents' lives as well. In fact, the degree of closeness felt by older generations is frequently stronger than the degree of closeness felt by younger generations. This may be because older persons view their children and grandchildren as their "legacy" or feel that the achievements of these younger relatives reflect positively on them and are a source of self-esteem.

PURPOSES, RESPONSES, STEPS, AND STRATEGIES

Holidays

Amanda was a single woman in her forties. She was fairly successful in business, but her parents, who were somewhat traditional in their beliefs, had difficulty accepting that she was not married and a mother. She felt that they did not respect her and showed little interest in her work and life.

Every year, her parents held a family gathering on Christmas Day. It was one of the few times the whole family was together for a joyous occasion, but Amanda felt tension, distance, and a sense that her parents were embarrassed by her, so she had avoided coming for two years. Finally, after some soul-searching, she decided that she wanted to be with the family but needed to clear things as best she could with her parents.

A week before the gathering, Amanda visited her mother to have a talk at a time when her mother was not busy preparing for the get-together. "Mother," she said, "I have not come to the family party for two years because I have felt that you have not taken any interest in my life and act like I'm not your child in front of the rest of the family. I am not going to be cut off from the rest of the family because of how you may feel about me." Her mother denied that this was so, but Amanda remained firm in saying that these were *her* perceptions and she was coming to the party to be with the family, two points that her mother could not contest.

Since that confrontation, her mother has begun to take more interest in her and, according to Amanda, has spent some time at the family party "listening in" on Amanda's conversations with other family members about what she was doing.

In some families, holidays are a time for great joy and caring. In most, there is a mixture of happiness and discomfort. They can also be a time of considerable stress, not only for the hosts (who will feel under the gun to have a good meal, make sure everyone is happy, and so forth), but for the rest of the family as well. Old conflicts may surface, there can be jockeying among siblings for status, there can even be competition about whose children are the "best" (behaved, achievers, students, athletes, performers). Parents will worry about how their children will act —will they be dutiful and loving to persons whom they are "supposed" to love, even though they may not know many of them well? Others will worry that whoever in the family has been on bad terms will make a scene and upset everyone else.

Against this background of concerns and hopes for a pleasant time, the following issues may emerge for children of elderly parents.

Shifting the Site of a Family Gathering. In some families, there is a fair amount of excuse-making to get a meal that has traditionally been held at a parent's house moved from the site because the parent is not, in the estimation of the family, capable of managing the meal. How you go about this depends upon the abilities of your parent, how the parent views her (usually it is a mother) abilities, and how the rest of your family communicates about similar issues.

If the amount of work involved in the meal is beyond the abilities of your parent (or if worrying about it would make the rest of you have a miserable time at the gathering), your mission is to get an agreement from your parent to participate in a new setting without getting "stuck" on the fact that she is not making the big family meal. There may be some strong sense of loss of both ability and the symbolic status of being the "chief cook." There may even be reminiscing during the current meal about previous times when meals were held at your parent's house. This can, depending on how the current decision was reached and how your parent does the reminiscing, be either comforting or distressing for the rest of the family.

You are faced with two approaches in getting this decision made. One is to bypass the truth of the matter and get your parent to agree with the "facts"—that your house is bigger, that another place is more central, that things will be "easier" and she can "relax" if the event is held elsewhere. At times, these reasons will make sense. But they can also seem somewhat empty and may be interpreted as a statement that your parent cannot handle herself as she used to and, more important, that you cannot talk to her about it because she is incapable of hearing the truth.

The second approach is to talk directly about what *you* want and need. That is, partly you want to feel comfortable and not worry about your parent (which is true), and partly you worry about the toll of the work of preparation on her (which is true). You may want to discuss how capable she is of making a big meal, but I would recommend first getting some recognition from her that it is a lot of work and then helping her separate her sense of self-esteem from the role of cook and hostess.

I do not, at the same time, recommend going into this discussion as if the decision were only your parent's to make. If you have already, in your heart, determined that a change will be made, then the decision is made. How you break the news and allow your parent to come to the same conclusion is the matter of strategy and timing and can have considerable variation, but making a decision appear to be unmade when it is will only lead you into trouble.

Time and timing are important in this issue. The longer you wait, the worse it will be. Consider how hard it could be to discuss changing Thanksgiving dinner after your parent has already bought the turkey! I prefer people to do these things face to face, but if you live far from your parent, you may have to do this work on the telephone. I recommend having more than one conversation, which will give your parent time to consider your concerns and any "facts" you may present. And for heaven's sake, be sure you are reassuring to your parent that your affection for them is unchanged.

Leaving Someone Out

> Steven and Hannah were the son and daughter-in-law of Tina, who was in her early eighties. Tina was frail and easily tired. Steven and Hannah had grown children of their own. Their youngest, Becky, who had two infants, wanted to have a party at her house with both sides of her family there, as she lived halfway between her parents and grandmother and her husband's parents and grandmother. However, if she had the party at her house, Tina would be left out since both she and her children felt she could not manage the four-hour drive each way.
>
> Steven and Hannah did not know what to do, because they feared that Tina would take everything personally if a party was held without her.

As complicated as this situation seems, it is not uncommon, as more and more three- and four-generation families exist. Logistics create situations that are "unworkable" in that everyone's wishes cannot be accommodated. In this particular situation, how Steven and Hannah talk with Tina will very much be influenced by how Tina views her situation, how they talk about other matters, their relationship, and their sense of self-esteem. In some circumstances, the children (e.g., Steven and Hannah) have been known to "sneak" a visit, not discussing it with their elderly parent. In others, they might not go, because of guilt about being with the family when their mother is not. In others, the children's guilt may lead to some rationalized discussion (for example, they may tell the elderly parent that they are going for a short visit that won't be fun because the in-laws will be there).

As hard as it may be, I feel strongly that it is best to be direct and gentle about the visit. Remember, if you choose to talk about it, that the decision has already been made, so you should not pretend that it is in process. At the same time, it may turn out that your parent is also torn between going and staying and needs some reassurance to feel good about not going (guilt works two ways). In some families, plans have been made to have second "holidays" at times convenient for members to be together (so Becky and her family come up for a second party at a later point when they can do so comfortably), but these will only work out when there is some talk about the sadness (on all sides) of not being together on the actual holiday or event, and no (or little) guilt about having a second event.

Going to "Other Family." Many children of older parents have family of a spouse as well as their own. At holiday times, it is natural to have a desire (or obligation) to spend time with both sides. On holidays such as Thanksgiving, which only allow one day (and when transportation is difficult to arrange), you may find yourselves torn between the two sides. Some families alternate, some try to get everyone together, and some actually go two places on the same day. You will, at times, have to choose one or the other. Note that this choice does not necessarily reflect your preference; I encounter far more families who try to be fair out of a sense of obligation or duty than those who choose to be with the relatives they like the most. In any case, the choice does have to be made.

How you talk to your parents who are being excluded is important. Avoiding the discussion will only allow any feelings of rejection to fester and come up later in indirect and destructive ways (as Lorry will eventually discover).

Your purpose in this type of discussion is to inform your parents of a decision and reassure them that you love them and that this is not a sign that you are abandoning them. At the same time, you will be decreasing the guilt of avoiding the topic when you finally talk about it openly and directly.

When Your Parent Is in an Institution. Holidays are particularly painful for residents of institutions who do not have family contact at such times, in part because they will see other residents being taken out, having a special meal or visit, or seeming to be happy with their family situation. (I say "seeming" because some residents may alter the truth to gain status and maintain self-esteem.)

If you are unable to include your institutionalized relative in a special event, it is an issue worth discussing. This is particularly important because some older persons will not raise the subject with their children. After all, they may wonder, if their children are so insensitive as to ignore them on the holidays, what good would it do to talk to them about it?

I think it is useful to have these discussions, as painful as they may be and even if you believe that your parent will forget what you say (which may well be true). The reasons are simple. First, it gives your parents the opportunity to know why you are not celebrating the event with them. Second, you can offer reassurance to decrease your parents' sense of being abandoned. Finally, as was mentioned before, it can decrease your own guilt to be straight with your parents.

Handling Obligations. At holiday time there is a strong sense of obligation to show up at a family gathering and endure aspects of the gathering that you do not like or feel uncomfortable about, in part because you do not want to make things difficult for others (which is very close to placating), or because you are willing to live with some discomfort for the short period of time you are all together. This was the situation faced by Amanda, who chose to develop a sophisticated (and effective) strategy for handling the negative parts of her holiday obligations.

Gifts

Debra was the mother of Prentice and Adrianne. Both Prentice and Adrianne had young children. When exchanging gifts with family members on holidays, Debra would comment to Prentice's wife and children about how expensive the gifts she had received from Adrianne's family were. Occasionally she made similar comments to Adrianne and her children about Prentice's family. After a few years of this, Prentice and Adrianne discovered while talking together that their mother had been playing them against each other, with resulting guilt and bad feelings growing between them.

Kathy was a widow who was quite well off yet refused to spend any money on herself beyond a few basic items. Her daughters, Darlene and Moira, knocked themselves out giving nice gifts to their mother, only to find that Kathy would returned them to the store. (Kathy was quite resourceful: even when the labels were cut from clothing, she invariably found the store or one that would accept the dresses as a return.)

Rather than stay hung up on the gift issue, Darlene one day asked her mother what she would like for a gift. "I still like books," her mother replied. Darlene then made it her business to buy Kathy books and gave up on using gift-giving occasions as the "opportunity" to try to alter her mother's wardrobe. Moira, however, continued to give her mother household items, clothing, and luxury items, and to remain frustrated when they were returned.

These two stories touch on several aspects of gift-giving. Even with the best of intentions, Prentice and Adrianne kept themselves in a guilt-ridden situation much longer than they had to (remember it took several years before they realized what was going on) because they did not communicate together about the situation or stand up assertively to their mother. Moira, on the other hand, was caught up in an ineffective way of using gifts to give her mother what she (Moira) wanted her mother to have—ineffective since her mother refused to keep the gifts.

Usually we think of gifts as symbolizing love and affection from one person to another. At the same, time, gift-giving is fraught with potential snags. In some families, it is important to give or receive the most expensive gifts, as somehow the price of the gift represents how much one loves or is loved. (This phenomenon has serious financial consequences, as anyone who has created great debts during the Christmas season knows.) In other families, it is very important that the gift be the "right" one for the recipient, because if it is wrong, that means that one is not loved or does not love enough.

With older relatives, other uncomfortable situations can arise. Sometimes an older relative spends so much on children and grandchildren that the recipients feel awkward about receiving the presents. Or the older relative gives away his or her own possessions as presents, which can be distressing to family members who see this as a sign of their parent's giving up on life. A third example is the older relative who refuses gifts from family. A fourth is the older person who does not give gifts at all. This can be especially upsetting to younger children, who feel bad when their birthday has been overlooked by a grandparent.

Each of these situations create guilt and concern for family members. If you choose to talk with your parent about the situation, the key issue is how to talk about it so as to produce a more comfortable state of affairs.

Presents are difficult to talk about, particularly if you have received an unwanted gift from a parent who is obviously emotionally invested in the gift. I think there is considerable leeway about accepting gifts that are not perfect and, to a lesser degree, gifts that are too extravagant. However, if you are concerned about what the overspending on gifts means, then you had better discuss it directly (preferably in between gift-giving times, when there is a reasonable chance the next gift has not yet been bought). If you are dealing with an older person who gives things away, you will have to weigh being gracious and taking the gifts as an expression of affection (and feeling okay about putting them in an attic or however you dispose of them) against talking about your concerns over what the giving away means to your parent.

A secondary but important concern arises if you feel that guilt or uncomfortable feelings are attached to the gifts. Sometimes such guilt is individually tailored; at other times it reflects a family pattern, as was the case for Debra, Prentice, and Adrianne. A common source of discomfort comes when a parent gives middle-aged children money for anniversaries or birthdays and the children feel that the parent is trying to control them or is stating that they are not self-sufficient. The only way out of this is to take the risk of sharing feelings, discussing what you want, and working together on how gifts are given. Otherwise, you will be left feeling bad no matter how you handle it. (Remember the story of Caroline in Chapter 9; she was gradually giving her estate away, and everyone felt bad until they learned her reasons for doing so.)

Talking about Other Family Members

> Marjorie was 48, a single working parent. Her mother, Josephine, was 79. Marjorie had had counseling and was beginning to appreciate some of the pain and suffering in her family's past. In a spirit of wanting to share with her mother, one day she said, "You know, Mother, our family had some pretty crazy times." Her mother turned to her, looked directly in her eye, and, with finger pointing directly at her, said, "How *dare* you say that? It was wonderful. Don't you ever disgrace the memory of your beloved father by ever saying that again!"

Marjorie was put in the same position as Bill in the beginning of this chapter. It was clear that each of their mothers had strong feelings about other family members who were not present and that these feelings were not shared by their children. At the same time, neither mother was terribly open to hearing a difference of opinion.

In many families, there is a natural tendency to talk about other family members, their lives, and other family "gossip" or information. If you share your parents' viewpoint, the discussions will go smoothly, with you being in perfect accord about who is doing well, who should be ashamed of themselves, who had something nice happen to them, who had something humorous happen, who is a star, and who is no good.

Families being what they are, however, you, may find that your views of the rest of the family differ considerably from those of your parents. At times you may find yourself compelled to disagree with a parent as to what went wrong and who is at fault. You may also find yourself wanting to defend a family member to your parent, as Brandy did in the beginning of this chapter.

There are no hard and fast rules about how to talk about other family members. At times, adult children choose to ignore comments. Others choose to set specific limits—for example, they will not listen to gossip about or putdowns of others during visits with their parents. The ability to comment about the situation (meta-commenting) is, obviously, an important skill in talking about other family members.

In the case of Marjorie, the situation is more complicated because Marjorie has gained some appreciation of her family, but her mother does not want to hear it. At the same time, it could also be that her mother is reacting to the word "crazy" and Marjorie could continue the discussion but translate potential red-flag words into ones without a stigma. For instance, she could say, "Our family had its share of struggles" instead of "Our family had some pretty crazy times." At the same time, if you find yourself getting a response like Josephine's (including the blaming finger and the elevation of a family member to sainthood), you should also be prepared for a lack of insight into the family and strong denial of family problems by your parent.

Being a Peacemaker

You might find yourself in the position of having to make peace or improve relationships between your parent and another family member. For example, you may need to intercede on behalf of a family member, to persuade two feuding relatives to be physically present with each other, or to get your parent to refrain from venting negative reactions to a relative (as Brandy did with her mother at the start of this chapter).

If you are interceding as a peacemaker, your role needs to be carefully circumscribed: that is, you shouldn't do others' work for them. You cannot guarantee that people will behave well when they are together, neither can you guarantee that things will be better as a result of the peacemaking effort. You can, however, reassure people that there is goodwill on all sides, that there are *potential* benefits of trying to make peace, and that taking risks is an admirable step. Of course, you cannot force your parent to make peace with another family member, but you certainly can express your disappointment about the situation (without pressuring them to agree out of guilt to a meeting that is bound to fail).

A final consideration about the peacemaker role is the problem of triangulation. Triangulation means that you are drawn into two other people's problems as a third "leg," which in turn leads to an unpleasant situation for all three of you. The general advice is to avoid triangulation or, if you are in it, to get out of the role of being the third leg.

A final purpose in talking about the family, its past, or even deceased family members is to help your parent reach some resolution and growth about his or her family concerns. You can be a sounding board, voice of reason, or concerned listener as your parent tries to put his or her life together. If you choose to do this, you must be careful to avoid taking sides, giving advice, offering opinions, or otherwise unduly influencing your parent. If you have things that "must" be said, be sure that you understand the difference between helping your parent and helping yourself before saying them.

I am not recommending that all families take upon themselves the responsibility for helping their parents make peace for themselves about their past. However, few older person get involved in formal mental health services with this goal, and few mental health professionals are interested in this area. Also, the discussions you have with your parent about the family and the past may have this purpose as an underlying theme, and it is one that is worth considering.

SOME CONSIDERATIONS IN TALKING ABOUT THE FAMILY

Several themes in this chapter involve how to approach the multiple concerns you have about talking with your parents about your family. The major ones are these:

- Own your own feelings (use "I" statements).
- Appreciate your own family's rules and norms about communication. Some may have to be addressed directly with your parent or with other family members before the discussion you want to have.
- Be careful. There will be misunderstanding, differing views, and many other issues that come up in discussions about family matters.
- Expect feelings and self-worth to be highly involved in these discussions on all parts, including yours.
- Ignore guilt thrown your way (and it will be if you disagree about central concerns or are perceived as being neglectful or abandoning your parent).
- If you feel the need to speak out about an issue, do it well: be assertive, specific, and clear.

- Allow time for your views to sink in or for decisions to be worked through.
- An alternative: Consider calling on outside help (other family members, professional family counselors or therapists) if your discussions are only making things worse for all of you.

RESOURCES

Hooyman, N. R., and W. Lustbader. *Taking Care: Supporting Older People and Their Families.* New York: Free Press, 1986. This book, designed as a textbook for professionals, offers a wealth of information, strategies, and ideas on many aspects of dealing with older relatives. It is a good supplement to this book and is noted in several other chapters.

Nerin, W. F. *Family Reconstruction: Long Day's Journey into Light.* New York: W. W. Norton, 1986. This book, focusing on how family history can be replayed for psychological growth and benefit, should be of some interest to you in uncovering issues in your and your parents' past. It can also give you insight into how you and other family members operate the way you do together.

Satir, V. *Peoplemaking.* Palo Alto, Calif.: Science and Behavior Books, 1972. This book, mentioned earlier, is a wonderful reference for examining how you communicate in families and how to appreciate your family dynamics and family communication.

15
Talking about You

Norma, 79, who lives in Florida and is quite well off, comes to visit her middle-aged daughter, Beverly, for two weeks every spring. As soon as Norma arrives, she starts taking over the responsibility of cooking and cleaning. She also, according to Beverly, continuously tells her what to do, what to wear, and so forth, much as she directed Beverly when she was much younger. Beverly puts up with it, feeling that two weeks is a short enough time to endure it, but she also realizes that they have at least one drawn-out, drag-down fight during each visit as well. In addition, Beverly feels that her mother is creating a bad relationship with her grandchildren.

Donna, 38, and her husband are from a small town in Illinois, near where his firm is based. They have been living on the West Coast for several years, and he is due to be transferred back home. Donna dreads the move because she will be the only member of her generation in the family who lives in their hometown, where both her parents and her in-laws, in their seventies, and two grandparents, in their late eighties, live. Donna knows that she will bear the brunt of taking care of all of them and is depressed about the prospect of spending the next twenty years looking after older relatives rather than living her own life. (She also has two children, and she worries about how much time she will have for them, as at least two of the elderly members of her family need constant attention at present).
   Donna also feels that she cannot discuss these matters with any of the parents or grandparents, as they will only think she is being selfish and rejecting them, which is not the case.

MaryAnne has recently separated from her husband of ten years. Her parents are upset about it and urge her to get back together with him "for the sake of the children." MaryAnne wants to return to work full-time as a fashion buyer. Her parents invite her for dinner on what would have been her tenth anniversary. She knows they will put pressure on her to try to get back with her husband and doesn't know what to say to them.

These three situations are not uncommon. Beverly, trying to be a dutiful child, chooses to put up with her mother's "parenting" for a two-

week visit rather than take the risk of working for a more mature relationship. Donna feels trapped by what she sees is an unfair obligation
that will be thrust upon her, perhaps for decades, and that she has little
opportunity to discuss. MaryAnne is torn between love for her parents,
guilt over the divorce, and knowing what she needs for herself. Each of
them, while perhaps choosing to be silent about her situation, should at
least consider the potential risks and gains to be made from beginning
to talk about herself, her needs and wishes, and her desire to be a caring
family member.

This chapter focuses on you, on what you want, what you need, and
what you want to say to your parents. It is put last because in a way, all
of the chapters in this book are about you. You are the one who is taking
the time to consider some new options for talking to your parents; you
are the one who may take some risks to promote positive changes; you
are the one who is choosing to stay with some difficult circumstances;
you are the one who has some hope for good feelings and connections
with older relatives. You are also more than a child of an elderly parent.
Your other roles may include being a worker, spouse, parent, brother or
sister, neighbor, and friend. Your needs have to be part of how you relate
and talk with your parents.

One of the themes that has run through the other chapters in this
book is how you can make your wishes and concerns known to your
parents. Frequently, I have urged you to use "I" language; be direct and
assertive; avoid blaming, placating, or defensive behavior; and listen to
the reactions of your parents as they attempt to listen to you. The same
general set of guidelines holds for talking about yourself.

Talking about yourself can be confusing in that it is closely related to
talking to your parents about your concerns about them, about other
family members, and your past. It is extremely useful to sort out the
pieces of discussion that are "you" from the pieces of discussion that are
"them." Otherwise, guilt and a certain lack of clarity about whom the
discussion is really for will come about, with subsequent difficulties in
defining problems and resolving them.

Part of the confusion comes from the fact that you are dealing with
your parents. Parents and children, along with being important parts of
each other's lives, usually have long histories of misgivings, unfinished
business, unresolved conflicts, and misunderstandings, along with good
feelings, a sense of connectedness, and pleasure in each other's company.
All of these attributes exist in any parent-child relationship to some

degree. It is the blending of resolved and unresolved issues, your current situation with your parents, and your own sense of growth and change that result in your current relationship with your parents.

Communication is the bridge between people. The skills and considerations I have been describing and illustrating in this book are tools by which you can help improve relationships, decrease misunderstanding, decrease calibration cycles, and work with your parents to help them meet some of their own needs. However, using effective communication also relies on you to appreciate and understand yourself, your own varying motivations, and your own communication styles at various times. It will not be enough for you to find a few skills and ideas on how to approach certain problems with your parents. After the beginning, the first "real" conversations, you will find that you want more, for both your benefit and your parents'. This chapter is the beginning of this second level— beginning to relate more fully to your parents as individuals and improving the chances that they will do the same to you.

SOME FACTS AND FIGURES ABOUT YOU

Who are you? What makes you different? What makes you a unique person? The answers to these questions lie with you as an individual. I can, however, tell you several things that are likely to be true about you as a reader of this book.

For Women

First, you are likely to be over the age of 30. (This conclusion comes from knowing that most caregivers of the elderly are women, and since most women now over 65 had children before the age of 35, that leaves you being over age 30.)

Second, you are likely to be working. As of 1986, more than half of the women in the United States were in the labor force.

Third, you are likely to feel pulled by several obligations, including family (your husband and children if any), your elderly parents, work, community obligations, and the needs of your husband's older family members.

Fourth, you are pulled by various role expectations, some of which do not fit you and members of your generation very well, such as feeling that you should stay home and take care of older relatives.

Fifth, you are uncomfortable with some aspects of the current state of affairs with your older relatives. You know there must be a better way but have not yet found one that is totally satisfactory for you. If you have read the rest of this book before reading this chapter, I hope that you have found some situations that resemble your own as well as some that do not apply to you (after all, who needs *all* the troubles of the world?).

For Men

A generation ago, there would have been very few men reading this book. You are still unusual if you are taking the time to read this. Most of the responsibilities for the emotional aspects of dealing with older relatives have traditionally fallen to women. Hopefully, this will change as we all take equal responsibility with our parents. At the same time, you may be trying out ways of relating to the world and of handling feelings that are different from what you were brought up to expect. This means that some of your attempts to make change will be shaky if they are not well integrated into your own psyche.

Many men enter the arena of dealing with elderly parents by addressing specific logistical or financial issues, such as change of residence, making a will, financial planning, or institutionalization. However, the emotional issues are still there for all of us. It may be less common for men to talk with their parents about their personal lives and human needs than for women, but that does not mean it is any less important. Some of the research being done on sex roles in society suggests that a balance of both traditional masculine attributes (assertiveness, instrumentality) and feminine attributes (nurturance, self-expression) is healthy and useful for both sexes and can be accomplished without jeopardizing one's identity as a man or woman.

As a man who may have a need to talk about himself to his parents, you are in the interesting situation of doing something that many men in your parents' generation neither did nor expected from other men— that is, talking about their inner needs and wishes. As you venture forth into this area, you will find puzzlement, misunderstanding, and perhaps genuine interest and curiosity from your parents about what is going on for you to do these "new" things. It will take time for your message to sink in, but, I believe, there will be potential benefit to both you and your parents in your doing so.

For Everybody

There is a kind of behavior I have recommended so much that I almost fear I have overstated my case; yet it is behavior that does not seem to be commonly practiced by many people in dealing with their elderly parents: that is, *direct, nondefensive, and personal communication* (and connections) between you and your parents. Without this approach, you are not likely to positively influence important issues (your relationship, your parents' situation, and so forth).

This point is made carefully: it is *possible* for your parents to change their ways without your help (as it is for you to change without theirs), but if you want to have influence *or* you want the relationship between you and your parents to change, then you have to start the ball rolling. It is not enough to wish that *they* will change. You have to do something, even if it is as subtle as establishing hope, refusing to feel guilty when guilt is thrown your way, or refusing to argue futilely as you may have done in the past.

This chapter, then, is primarily for you. It covers several aspects of what you may be talking to your parents about, but in each case the underlying goal is that you want to feel better about something and you want your own sense of self-worth and confidence to grow. The topics covered here are among those most frequently encountered by children of the elderly as they work in the direction of their own growth.

PURPOSES, RESPONSES, STEPS, STRATEGIES, AND OUTCOMES

Your Children

Tanya was the daughter-in-law of Katy, a woman in her early sixties who had always been the matriarch of her family. Whenever Katy visited her grandchildren, she took it upon herself to discipline them and show them the correct way to behave, using an authoritative manner and a pointing finger. Jeff, Tanya's husband and Katy's son, handled this by telling his wife to go along with it and that there was not much they could do about it, as Katy had always been like that.

Tanya, having a mind of her own, felt that things had to change, in part because she knew her children were becoming disenchanted with their grandmother.

At last, Tanya sat down with Katy and had a long discussion about her life, her husband, and her children.

"You know," she said, finally leading up to the main point, "you had to work hard to raise Jeff and his sister. You don't have to work that hard now as a grandparent. Let us handle the hard work of discipline. I know we do it differently than you did, but that's our job. Let your time be remembered by them as good times rather than discipline. If you have a concern, tell us, not them, okay?"

Katy agreed and subsequently changed the way she interacted with the grandchildren. Of course, she would continue to "discuss" how Tanya raised the children with Jeff (and occasionally and indirectly with Tanya), but from the viewpoint of the grandchildren, Grandma had undergone a miraculous transformation. For Jeff and Tanya, it was enough to make this change. They chose not to confront Katy about her guilt-inducing manner with them.

This story highlights the bonds and complications of talking with your parents about your children. Although your children are also part of the rest of the family, you naturally fall between them and your parents. In addition, bonds on both sides are usually stronger than bonds between other family members.

The types of concerns that come up in talking to your parents about your children include how you are raising them, what they are doing or accomplishing, setting limits on what your parents do with your children (especially in the discipline department), arranging time for them to be together, and discussing how your parents and children relate to each other. In the case of Tanya and Katy, Tanya chose to talk with Katy to set limits on Katy's interaction. She also did it in a positive manner and paved the way for positive interactions between grandmother and grandchildren in the future.

A related issue is how or whether to prepare your children for interaction with their grandparents. Many parents would claim that they do not need to "prime" their children for this. I would agree, especially if the emotional bonds are strong and the interaction goes smoothly. At the same time, if the grandparent has a particularly disabling condition or lives in a nursing home where children may observe things that could frighten them, some preparation and debriefing *after* a visit may be called for. Children may need to understand why their grandparent has trouble hearing or seeing, or may need to be told why an Alzheimer's patient forgets the children's names (so that the children won't feel slighted or think it's because the grandparent is "old").

Less frequently, a grandparent has a particular style of relating that parents want to "protect" their children from. If this is your situation,

I would prefer your handling it as Tanya and Katy did instead of avoiding the problem by not visiting your parents or telling your children to ignore them. Although dismissing the grandparent's behavior to the children may seem the easiest solution, in doing so you are running the risk of making things worse for both child and grandparent as well as potentially drawing the grandchild into your own difficulties with your parent as the third leg of an uncomfortable triangle.

In talking to your parents about your children, you will also do well to realize that grandchildren represent an extension of self for many grandparents. It will be hard for them to hear news about an illness or a hospitalization. At the same time, shielding your parents from bad news has the same potential consequences as shielding them from other types of information as has been discussed in earlier chapters of this book. You should carefully weigh what information you withhold. I think most people conceal too much, because they assume that averting their parents' expected reaction is worth the suspicion that the deception is bound to arouse. I can understand why families shield their elders from some bad news, but I also believe that they frequently underestimate the abilities of their older relatives to handle it.

Your Career

Parents have a natural interest in their children's work. If you are a son, it is usually a question of how you are "succeeding" in your job. If you are a daughter, there may be a mixture of responses, including pride in your accomplishment; disdain if you are seen as working at the "expense" of your children, or if you are unmarried; envy for opportunities you enjoy that were not available to your elderly mother in the past; wondering about how you are fulfilling the role of wife, or not exactly understanding what it is you do (since women are assumed to undertake only certain jobs in the labor force). These reactions can come out in a range of ways, direct or indirect, and can be complicated by issues that are raised when your work may interfere with meeting obligations to care for your parents. At the same time, your parents may also have an understanding of issues that far surpasses your expectations, as in the following story.

Denise, 35, was the daughter of Ronald, a widower in his eighties. She had quit her job as an insurance underwriter to care first for her mother, who had died ten years earlier, and now for her father, who shared his home with her. However, after ten years, Denise felt that her father's condition (which was deteriorating), their financial situation (which was becoming precarious), and her own future needs for employment warranted her getting back into the job market at least on a part-time basis. Her earnings would pay for a health aide to be in the house when she was working or taking care of her personal business, not to mention trying to revive her poorly developed social life.

Denise could not, however, bring herself to tell her father that she was taking a job to prepare for the future or to take time for herself. After talking with several people, including her minister, she got up the courage to talk with her father. To her great surprise, he understood her needs for time for herself and actually welcomed having someone else in the house to talk to, after being reassured that Denise was not abandoning him.

Denise's situation was similar to Amanda's in the last chapter, in that both needed to take a stand on having a work life outside of traditional roles for women. Both used assertion and took time to talk about the issues with their parents. Their success (which was less immediate in Amanda's situation) depended on both their use of skills and the receptivity of their parents.

There are, of course, no guarantees about how your parents will react when you talk to them about your job plans. If you are going back to work after having taken care of them in the past, the more you are sure of your own motivation (i.e., that the decision is right for you and you have little guilt about it) and the more you are not depending upon their approval for your decision, the easier time you will have talking about it, no matter what their response is.

Talking about Your Marriage, Divorce, or Remarriage

Audrey was in her late thirties and had two boys, ages 13 and 9. She had been feeling upset about her relationship with her husband for several years, and the tension in the house had become unbearable for all of them. There was little question that a separation and probable divorce were on the way, even after time spent in marital counseling.

Audrey had chosen to keep her difficulties from her parents, who really liked her husband. Finally, however, her parents came to visit for Christmas. Not surprisingly, Christmas dinner was uncomfortable for everyone. The next day, Audrey suggested to her mother that they go shopping together, an activity they had enjoyed in the past.

After they got out of the car and while they were walking through the somewhat crowded stores, Audrey turned to her mother and said, "There's something I want to tell you. Bob and I are not doing well together. I think we are going to separate for a while."

Her mother, who ordinarily was a demonstrative person, was a bit subdued since they were in public. She began to tell Audrey that she should never separate from a husband, that the children would not have a good home, that there would be no money, and all of the other reasons people have for telling couples to stay together.

Audrey, who had been prepared for such a speech, listened quietly for a minute or two. "Mom," she finally said, "that's enough for now. I am not telling you this for you to give me advice. I am telling you this for information. It will be hard for me; it will be hard for the kids. I only hope you can stand by me during these difficult times."

Audrey reported that her parents both continued to have difficulty with her separation and subsequent divorce, and that she had to continually remind them that their role was to be supportive, not to give advice. She also had to be assertive when they gave little hints that they disapproved, by telling them that what they were saying was not helpful and that she needed their support (*not* their approval). Although this parent-child relationship was not the best, Audrey was able to prevent her parents from making her feel more upset than she already did during her divorce.

Both Audrey and MaryAnne (whose story was described in the beginning of this chapter) had to struggle with both their pain and the pain their parents had about their marital difficulties. In neither case did they feel that their parents were supportive. The key question for each was how to protect herself from parental response and pressure. In other cases, parents can be strong sources of support if their children have marital difficulties.

Families vary considerably in how much family members talk to others about their marital concerns. You may talk little to your parents about your marriage. You may talk a great deal, feeling there is benefit. You may also find yourself listening to your parents give advice, manipulate you, or otherwise communicate in ways that are not pleasant to receive. As a rule of thumb, the more you are uncomfortable with how your parents talk (or avoid talking) with you about your marriage, the more difficult it will be for you to talk to them about it, including giving them important information (such as news of your separation, marriage, or remarriage).

At the same time, events such as getting married or separated cannot escape parental attention forever. The issue in part is what to discuss and when to discuss it. I think some children wisely put off the discussions of marital difficulties because they find that the advice they have gotten from their parents in the past only makes them feel guilty or inadequate, or at best confuses them.

Even when you expect the worst kind of response from your parents to your news, and even when you get the worst, there is something to be said for being calm, keeping your self-esteem out of the way of their response, not being defensive, and standing your ground. Remember, when you drop any personal news, there is going to be an emotional reaction from the other person. While they may have some inkling things are moving in the direction you are discussing, it will still be their first encounter with all the forces you have been contending with for days, weeks, or months that led up to the current discussion.

What You Want for You and Them

> Shelly was the daughter of Mae, a widow in her mid-seventies. Mae had inherited a moderate estate but refused to spend any of the principal and only used the interest money as was absolutely needed. When Shelly talked to her about it, Mae would only say that she had to be sure there was enough for a "rainy day." Shelly spent futile hours arguing with Mae about how the estate was hers to spend, that it was useless to save for a catastrophic illness, since a prolonged hospitalization or institutionalization would wipe out her savings anyway. Mae listened politely and refused to spend money on herself.
> Shelly, in desperation, spoke to her husband and other family members about her concerns. Once, while talking with her aunt Juliette, Juliette happened to remember a conversation she and Mae had had thirty years ago, when Mae talked about her fears that the Great Depression would return and that she had to have enough saved up for that "rainy day."

It was only after the talk with Juliette that Shelly had a handle on what was behind her mother's resistance to spending money on herself. Shelly then decided that it was too difficult to convince her mother that the rainy day would never happen, and learned to live with her mother's decision without guilt or remorse over not having tried "everything" to give her mother peace of mind in her old age.

What you want for your parents may be physical (e.g., living situation) or psychological (e.g., less depression); it can represent a change in life-style, such as spending money saved during a lifetime; it can be for better relationships with others. Whereas some of the parts of this topic (a change in residence, better relationships with others) have been discussed earlier, this section will focus on changing life-styles and what you want emotionally from your parents.

Changing Your Parents' Life-Style. Children of the elderly sometimes wish their parents enjoyed themselves more, spent more money on themselves, or took advantage of certain programs or activities during their later years. These matters have been discussed in earlier chapters but bear restatement: in part, your discussion will hinge on the underlying motivation behind your desire to have your parents change and their underlying motivation for living the way they do. How much is their motivation related to unrealistic fears? How much is merely a continuation of previous patterns of behavior? What are the risks for change? What are the potential advantages and disadvantages? To what degree is either of you motivated by guilt or mistrust about past experiences either individually or together?

Some of the underlying motivation may come from what have been called generational differences; that is, events in the lives of your parents have motivated them to act in certain ways that make little or no sense to you. This was so for Mae in the case discussed above. Other parts may be too difficult or painful for you to address easily. Still others may be changed with cooperation and decisions coming from your parents. The bottom line is that your parents have the right to participate or not in activities and, in some sense, they have the right *not* to pursue happiness or peace of mind, although I urge you to encourage them to pursue these ideals.

Changing the "Tyrant." One of the topics that comes up with some regularity in discussions of older parents is the question of how to handle the parent who has been "tyrannical," that is, domineering, vindictive, critical, or guilt-inducing. You will know if your parent is like this almost without my saying anything about it, but for the benefit of the uninitiated, the following types of interactions and behaviors go with the so-called tyrannical parent:

- Much blaming of others for problems
- The ability to fly into rage easily, along with the use of a pointing finger and hostile body language, facial expressions, and posturing

- Blowing "hot and cold" (i.e., the person can be conciliatory, even placating after raging, without directly apologizing or recognizing his or her own behavior)
- Threatening to your self-esteem (and guilt-inducing) through the use of phrases such as "How *dare* you!," "Don't be so sensitive," "How could you do this to me?," and "I don't care what you say, I'm still your parent and I know what's best."
- Little self-awareness and frequent denial of her or his own temper, outbursts, and how he or she comes across to others (who usually think the outbursts are premeditated)

To some degree, you will have internalized your tyrannical parent's blaming into your sense of guilt. That is, for all the *wrong* reasons, you believe that, at some level, you are the cause of their problems and then let their "hooks" get into you, resulting in your heightened guilt and discomfort. Your parent, on the other hand, is likely to feel unloved and quite needy, and actually has a quite shaky sense of self-confidence. This may even be aggravated by the losses in self-esteem, status, and physical ability that may come with aging. Your parent may not know this is underlying his or her behavior, and is certainly unaware of the impression it makes on others.

Assuming that you can work on decreasing your own sense of guilt and begin to get out of the calibration cycles with your parent (not an easy task and one most people do not finish), you are still faced with a difficult situation in that your parent is unaware of both the behavior and the underlying dynamics. To simply state what your parent is doing will be greeted with disbelief or even rage (after all, it will be perceived as an attack).

At least initially, a far better "package" of communication strategies to *start* you on the road of talking with a tyrannical parent is the following:

- Determine which specific words, actions, aspects of speech (such as tone of voice), or body language is "tyrannical", controlling, guilt-inducing, and so forth. (This is similar to the first step in breaking other calibration cycles.)
- Work on learning how to say specifically what you are having trouble with and how it affects you: for example, "When you say that, I feel you are giving me no choice in the matter" or "By saying it that way, you're telling me that you don't love me if I don't go along."

- Work on saying specifically what you want: for example, "I want to have a say in the matter" or "I am going to make a choice here" or "Let's both discuss what we want in this case and decide together" or "I want love, with no strings attached and [as reassurance] I want to give love the same way."

- Be prepared to respond continually to each specific instance of tyranny by calmly stating your reaction and your request for what you want or need. You will be dealing with a shaky personality to begin with, and it can take considerable time to get even a small change for the better.

- You may get the "cold shoulder" from the tyrant in response to your requests for change. You can have some handy meta-comments available that point this out and open the door for future communication of a more positive nature: for example, "I sense that you're hurt and pulling away from me. That's okay. When you're ready to talk about it, we'll try again."

- Finally, practice what you are going to say with another person *before* you say it to your parent. Have the other person try to make you feel guilty, and *practice* avoiding guilt by doing the following (repeatedly):

  1. Taking a deep breath each time the guilt starts to rise
  2. Relaxing tight places in your body by consciously tightening and loosening them for about five seconds each
  3. Picturing a relaxing scene and entering it in your mind's eye each time the guilt starts to rise up
  4. Having some assertive, true, nonblaming responses that you can say, such as, "Mom, I don't understand what you want"; "I know you're angry and frustrated, but don't take it all out on me; that's not fair"; or "I want to understand you, but all I get is anger. What else are you feeling?"

Remember, the purpose of these suggestions is to get you involved in a positive communication cycle rather than the calibrative cycles you have had in the past. You may get no further than being able to state your feelings or wants without feeling guilty. Your parents may remain just as tyrannical as ever, with all their own guilt and low self-esteem intact. You may have to accept this as their "choice." However, by using nondefensive communication with them, you will know that you are not contributing to their pain and suffering (and believe me, the tyrant suffers psychologically just as much as the victim), and should not feel as much guilt as you perhaps have in the past.

Setting Limits

> Allison, 72, had moved in with Nancy and Alfred, her daughter and son-in-law. Allison had had an active social life before her husband had died two years earlier. One of the issues that emerged when Allison moved in was that Nancy and Alfred felt obligated to include Allison in every social activity they had. Thus, every time they were invited out, Allison went with them. Alfred began to feel that he had little time with his wife, but Nancy felt that it was her obligation to make a social life for her mother.
>
> Alfred finally felt pushed into doing something different. He first talked with Nancy to inform her that he needed to set some limits on Allison's social interaction with them and then talked with Allison about how they would like to spend time with her as well as spend time without her. Allison, who was not initially happy about the discussion, was given time to think about things (there were no immediately pressing social situations coming up) and actually volunteered to baby-sit with the children the next time Nancy and Alfred were invited out.

There is no guarantee that trying to set limits will work as well for you as it did for Alfred. However, without some direct discussion about the issue, no change could even begin to occur.

Setting limits has been discussed throughout this book. Guilt, obligations, and a sense of responsibility make the balancing act between what you want for you and what you should do for your parents difficult to consider, much less achieve in a "correct" way. There are times when our own needs have to take precedence over the needs of others. The problem in figuring out those times is that guilt or others' views of what is "correct" interferes with giving appropriate weight to a sense of obligation, figuring out other obligations and deciding the best way to live for yourself.

Even if you have weighed your sense of competing obligations successfully, you may still have difficult talks with your parents about a change in commitment. Imagine the difficulties you could have telling parents who have been martyrs for others that you are not going to do the same for them.

So, then, what to do? Consider the following suggestions for talking about setting limits:

- Be specific about what the limits mean (e.g., number of visits, chores done or not done) rather than making general statements ("I'm not going to be as available as I was").

- Continually and accurately separate the question of love from the limits of the obligations (but do it positively rather than negatively; e.g., "I do love and care for you, *and* I'm doing some things for myself" rather than "This doesn't mean I don't love you").

- Have the support of other family members, including your spouse, especially those who may be present at these discussions. You need them to be reassuring and not sabotage your efforts.

- Be willing to listen (without judging or feeling guilty) to your parents' response to your setting limits. While it may be uncomfortable, it will build trust and their faith in you.

- When your parents are venting to you, give no advice and do not try to solve any problems right away.

Coming Clean

"Coming clean" means getting rid of old emotional baggage, breaking the bonds of parental approval and dependency, and making peace with your parents. Particularly relevant to these issues are the following comments, written by Willa, a friend of mine who read portions of this book:

> My parents are no longer living. One piece of advice I constantly give to friends is to clean up any unfinished business with parents while they are still alive. When a parent dies, one of the first thoughts is, "When was the last time I saw him? What did I say?" It is important to mend relationships with elders so that the survivors do not live the remainder of their lives tortured by guilt over a final argument or unkind word.

Mending relationships and working on the painful issues is never easy and is never guaranteed to work. But, as Willa reminds us, the pain does not leave if left unattended.

Sometimes opportunities open that adult children can either accept or overlook:

> Michael was the son of Estelle and Scott, who were both in their late sixties. Michael had not had any direct contact with his parents for over five years. When he came into town, Estelle would only find out

from one of Michael's friends, who would call to let her know how her son was doing. Estelle felt that it was something she had done or perhaps the influence of Michael's wife, Andrea, that led to this lack of contact. She struggled for some time over what to do and, finally, after taking a course in assertion for the elderly, decided to risk calling her son on the telephone.

As she placed the call, Estelle felt scared that she was going to be rejected. Her first words to Michael were "Please do not hang up. This is your mother. I want to know why you stay away from us."

Michael was faced with a difficult choice at that point. He had never intended to hurt his mother but had such a bad history with his father that he could not bear being with them. He made a split-second decision to level with his mother.

"Mom," he said, "it's not you. You know that I never got along with Dad. I don't like being with him. But I love you."

"I love you, too", she said, starting to cry.

"Don't cry," he answered.

"It's okay, it's okay," she said. "I know your father is hard to get along with. It's hard for me, too. But I really want to hear your voice and know you're all right."

They talked some more and decided that he would call her once a month to talk but that they would not deal with his father, nor would he visit the two of them.

This case is important for several reasons. First, while Michael vaguely knew that his mother might be upset, he had no way of knowing how open she was to hearing him say anything "bad" about his father. Second, when his mother made an overture, Michael took it up, rather than deciding this was a guilt ploy or some other form of manipulation. Third, everything did *not* turn out "happily ever after." Many of our discussions with our parents about the past and old hurts do not get "finally" resolved. The process of working on old business is frequently continual, but the partial gains may be more than worth the effort and risk (of being hurt, of being rejected, and so forth).

Making peace with your parent is a topic so broad and complicated that other entire texts have been written about it. (Some of these books are mentioned at the end of this chapter.) Many systems of psychotherapy and family counseling are based on the premise that psychological health comes from working through issues we have from our childhood with our parents. Some actually advocate dealing directly with one's parents now to overcome past problems that are made manifest in current day-to-day living. Others suggest that the turmoil we experience about our parents dwells within each of us and should be handled separately from the current realities of our parents and ourselves.

I agree in part with both these viewpoints. I feel that some personal concerns can be worked out without drawing your parents into them. In other cases, peace can be made directly with your parents about issues that are still troubling the relationship to this day. Your success will depend on the relationship, the willingness of the parties to participate in straightening out the past, your skills and strategies, and the time you can devote for these tasks.

As you begin to talk with your parents about housing, finances, health, social issues, family, and personal matters, you may well find yourself wanting to clean up the past with them, to straighten out misunderstandings, reestablish contact, or otherwise free yourself from the psychological pains you have been carrying around with you for all these years. You may want to straighten out old feelings about which child got more from which parent, which parent gave more to you, who did not give, how much you wanted approval for your achievements and did get it, how you felt pressured to choose a particular career or spouse, how sad you were when your parents were not present at particular events, how you felt that they did not pay attention to you, how upset you were at things they did, and so forth.

These discussions are worth having. At the same time, most people do not start having them spontaneously as their parents reach old age. It can take considerable time to set the stage for a discussion about "you" and "them" and unfinished business. Your discussions may focus initially on what is going to be discussed and why, to build up trust and some common understanding of the goal of the discussion. Your parents may be unwilling to do much discussion, or they may be more willing than you think, provided you come across in a nondefensive manner.

Another consideration is that you have to be able to listen to your parents to get *new* information that will give you an adult understanding of situations that did not make sense to you as a child or from your perspective in the family system. (As an example of this, consider how many children blame themselves for their parents' divorce or deaths and carry these feelings with them into adulthood. Having information about what else was going on in the family at the time can help you overcome any overpersonalization of what happened in your past.)

An additional consideration is that you have to approach this discussion as equals with your parents. A discussion to clear up the past is for both you and them. Neither of you is only or fully the "parent" and the other the "child." You are two (or three) adults trying to make sense of your pasts together—difficult process but one that can have rich rewards on all sides.

WHERE DO YOU GO FROM HERE?

We have reached the end of this book. I hope you have begun to ask yourself some useful questions about what you want or need to talk to your elderly parents about (your purpose), what their reaction to this type of discussion might be, what information you need in order to have the initial discussions, what ways are likely to work best for you in talking with them, and what you want to have come out of the discussions. I also hope that you have attempted to consider how *your* communication style, other family, and the feelings of your parents may enter into the talks you have.

At the same time, having one or even a series of discussions is frequently not enough to resolve all difficulties. This book is a beginning. There may have to be hard work to find a suitable living arrangement, supportive service, health provider, nursing home, or social activity. The references at the end of each chapter represent the next level of information and guides you may need as you take on the support of your aging parents as concerned family members. This book has offered some guidelines to help you carry out your caregiving obligations with a positive sense of self-esteem. Caring for other people is never easy; it is never a simple matter. It is, however, one of the ways in which we experience our humanness and can reach the highest levels of our own potential. My best wishes go to each of you in your work with your families as they age.

RESOURCES

Bloomfield, H. H., and L. Felder. *Making Peace with Your Parents.* New York: Ballantine, 1985. This popular personal growth text discusses how you can work out your "inner" issues about your parents to have more enriching relationships in your life. It has a humanistic ideology and includes some exercises you can go through to make peace with your parents.

Hooyman, N. R., and W. Lustbader. *Taking Care: Supporting Older People and Their Families.* New York: Free Press, 1986. Mentioned earlier, this is one of the best books on strategies for handling the multiple issues facing older persons. It includes handy checklists and ideas on dealing with difficult situations.

Nerin, W. F. *Family Reconstruction: Long Day's Journey into Light.* New York: W. W. Norton, 1986. This book, mentioned in the previous chapter, focuses on how we can make peace with our early family issues by reconstructing the past through techniques of psychodrama and role-playing.

Satir, V. *Making Contact.* Milbrae, Calif.: Celestial Arts, 1976. This book focuses on how we as humans can relate to others fully. It is a lovely companion piece to *Peoplemaking.*

INDEX